G000095686

OW TO ...   HOW TO ...   HOW TO ...

run a quality
self-catering
accommodation

Published by VisitBritain, Thames Tower, Blacks Road, London W6 9EL
Publishing Manager: Seth Edwards
Production Manager: Celine Gale
Typesetting: Keystroke, 28 High Street, Tettenhall, Wolverhampton
Printing and binding: Wace Ltd, Swindon
Cover design: Eugenie Dodd Typographics

Front cover image courtesy of britainonview.com
Written by: Christopher Howard and David Falk at East of
England Tourist Board

Important note: the information contained in this publication has been
published in good faith on the basis of information submitted to VisitBritain.
Whilst every effort has been made to ensure that this information is correct,
VisitBritain regrets that it cannot guarantee complete accuracy and all liability
for loss, disappointment, negligence or other damages caused by reliance
on the information contained in this publication, is hereby excluded. As
changes often occur after press date, it is advisable to confirm the
information given.

© British Tourist Authority (trading as VisitBritain) 2006

ISBN: 978-0-7095-8278-6

visit **Britain**
publishing

Contents

Chapter 1
First thoughts

The first chapter of this book will help you to decide whether setting up a self-catering business is the right decision for you and your family. It covers the various considerations that you need to take into account, as well as the initial pros and cons involved in operating a holiday let. It will help you to make an informed decision on whether this is the right step for you.

An introduction to self-catering

Self-catering is a growth industry. As well as demand from overseas, there has been a steady increase in the demand for domestic holidays in the UK, whether it is for the main holiday of the year or a second break. Activity-based holidays, relaxing weekends, off-season breaks and family gatherings have all helped to extend letting periods and create high demand in season and at other times of the year.

Properties vary considerably from picture-postcard thatched cottages and modern city centre apartments to more unusual properties, such as converted windmills, stately homes and castles. A self-catering unit can be located almost anywhere, from an isolated setting on the coast, or in the heart of the North York Moors, to central London. It can be owner managed or managed by an agency.

You may be thinking of starting a self-catering business or indeed may already operate one. Perhaps you have an annexe attached to your own property or maybe you have inherited a property located in another area. You may already own a second home that has been let to a tenant or is being used as your own family holiday home. You could be looking to purchase a property as an investment or as part of your pension or retirement, or perhaps you have redundant outbuildings that could be converted for letting. Any of the above examples could be developed for the holiday letting market, but there are many practicalities to consider.

Do you have the right skills?

In managing your own self-catering business you need to ask yourself whether you have what it takes to operate the business effectively and efficiently; will you have the commitment it requires and have you got the physical attributes to carry it out?

EMOTIONAL COMMITMENT

An obvious first question you need to ask yourself is whether or not you really like people. You may be fairly extrovert and friendly in most situations, but are you able to look after your guests without being too attentive, so that they begin to feel uneasy? Alternatively, can you put up with guests who constantly want to talk to you and ask for information and advice? Indeed, will you be able to handle any complaints you may receive, even if they appear unfounded or irrational, and handle difficult guests? These aspects need to be considered. As rare as they may be, difficult situations can arise and need to be handled tactfully.

You also need to ask yourself how operating the self-catering business may affect you and your family. If your property is located adjoining the holiday let, will your family mind losing their privacy? Will it restrict them from being themselves? Unless there is an enclosed garden for the guests, will they mind sharing their own garden?

PRACTICAL SKILLS

To manage bookings you will need an efficient administration system. You will be dealing with enquiries, sending out brochures and confirmation letters, taking deposits and chasing up outstanding balances. With some larger units, guests may expect to use credit cards, so you may need to set up a suitable system for taking payments. You will need to consider how you advertise and promote your property, and you will need to do some initial research to understand the market. As well as all this, you will need to keep detailed business accounts for tax purposes, as well as for evaluating the success of your business.

An introduction to self-catering

In addition, there will be the weekly cleaning, as well as routine deep cleaning and maintenance, including redecoration. If you have a garden, this will always have to be neat and well tended. There may also be emergencies to cope with, such as the plumbing or a broken washing machine.

Do you have the right skills?

- EMOTIONAL COMMITMENT

- PRACTICAL SKILLS

Is your holiday home suitable?

This section asks whether your property will work as a holiday home. Will it provide the flexibility to accommodate guests in comfort? Does it offer enough space for everyone, allow easy access, provide parking, and is it suitably located?

Is your holiday home suitable?

- WHAT INFLUENCES CHOICE?

- COST

- FACILITIES

- QUALITY

WHAT INFLUENCES CHOICE?

To start answering these questions it is worth considering why guests stay where they do. Consider the guests' rationale when it comes to choosing a self-catering property. For many guests their choice of property may be related to location, for others the main consideration may be cost, and for others it may be the size and facilities available. For most guests, however, the final decision will be a combination of all of these factors, plus the all-important consideration of quality.

We will look more closely at the issue of location in the next section. Here we will concentrate on how the cost, facilities and quality of your property can affect a guest's decision to book.

COST

Cost is usually a factor for guests when deciding on a self-catering holiday. Guests who are on a very tight budget are likely to be price-sensitive. For them, cost becomes the most important factor in choosing the property and they are likely to select the cheapest option available. But many guests are also price-conscious. Being price-conscious means that price becomes equated with quality, and other factors start to affect the decision. Some guests may be attracted to a higher price, some to a mid-price. Consider the last time you bought a pair of new shoes, or carpeted your home. Did the price you paid reflect the quality of your purchase? Very often price will reflect the standard of quality and the cheapest option is not always the preferred option. If the price seems too low, guests are likely to think that there may be a catch or that the quality is lower. If the price is too high, they may look elsewhere. Alternatively you may want to specifically target the higher end of the market where guests are willing to pay for a higher level of quality.

FACILITIES

Self-catering properties throughout the country offer a varied range of facilities from en-suite bathrooms to full leisure facilities. As living standards have increased, so too have guests' expectations. No longer is a black and white TV acceptable. Some guests will be used to en-suite bathrooms in their own homes, whilst families will be looking for spacious accommodation. If you have large grounds and gardens, guests may find this an added attraction.

It is essential at this stage to be aware of the Disability Discrimination Act (DDA). The DDA puts emphasis on ensuring services are *reasonably* accessible for all guests. Although primarily concerned with the requirements of those with a disability, there can be benefits for other guests and it can help to maximise the potential of your property. There is more information on the DDA in Chapter 2.

QUALITY

Whilst all of the above can influence the choice of where to stay, guests are also concerned about the quality of the accommodation they are about to book. Booking accommodation is an unusual purchase, as we are often buying something sight unseen. Unlike the last time you bought shoes, or purchased a carpet, you do not get the opportunity to see or try accommodation before deciding to make a booking.

When buying accommodation, you are committing yourself to spending money. How do you know your purchase will match your expectations? The best form of advertising a proprietor will ever have is by word of mouth. The customer chooses a self-catering holiday based on a trusted recommendation. That gives them some reassurance of the level of quality they will experience. But without word of mouth, how can guests know what quality to expect? The National Quality Assurance Schemes provide quality ratings that guests can use to make an informed and quality-assured decision on where to stay. We will focus on the National Quality Assurance Schemes (NQAS) in Chapter 5.

The aspect of quality comprises the main substance of this guide and will be assessed in more detail in later chapters.

Where is your property located?

The location of a self-catering property can vary considerably from a wing of your own home, to rural cottages, converted farm outbuildings and city centre apartments. The type of property you own will affect how you manage it and how it affects you and your family.

THE IMPORTANCE OF LOCATION

Choosing a self-catering property because of its location is often a guest's first priority. The need to be staying in or around the area may be dictated by the desire to visit a particular destination, but could also be affected by having to work in the area, attend an event or join a family gathering. Alternatively, for those guests on holiday or taking a short break, there may have been a choice of locations, and other considerations may have affected their final choice.

Being in the right location may seem a difficult point to consider. After all, you cannot move your property from what is perceived to be a difficult location. The main factor to consider here is whether or not your location will draw guests to you. What reasons will they have to be in your area? And what features or local places of interest could you use to promote your location as the one to choose over others?

A PROPERTY ADJOINING OR ADJACENT TO YOUR HOME

An adjoining or adjacent property could mean a cottage or units in the garden or grounds of your home, or sub-dividing your home so that it will lend itself to self-catering. Because

Is your holiday home suitable?
- WHAT INFLUENCES CHOICE?
- COST
- FACILITIES
- QUALITY

Where is your property located?
- THE IMPORTANCE OF LOCATION
- A PROPERTY ADJOINING OR ADJACENT TO YOUR HOME
- A DISTANT PROPERTY
- A SECOND HOME
- CONVERTING OUTBUILDINGS
- AN INVESTMENT PROPERTY

of the proximity of the self-catering property to your own home, you could be able to manage the property and all lettings yourself. The minus side to this is that you may lose some privacy. There may be some shared areas, such as your garden, and you will be committed to a changeover day (usually a Saturday), which can affect your social life. You may have to limit the time of year when you can take your own holidays to a 'quiet time' and, if you do go away, there is the potential loss of enquiries and bookings.

The plus side is that it will be less expensive than employing an agent, you will have complete control over standards of cleaning and maintenance, you will be able to meet your guests and you will be on hand for any problems that arise. You can also decide when you want to take guests and control your booking diary completely.

A DISTANT PROPERTY

You may live in one part of the country but own, or are about to purchase, a property suitable for holiday lets in a different part of the country. If this is the case, you will probably not be able to have personal contact with your guests, but you may still be able to manage bookings and enquiries. In this situation you will need to implement a suitable booking system able to cope efficiently and effectively with enquiries. You may be able to carry out annual spring-cleaning and complete some decorating and simple DIY jobs in the quiet season. But for the weekly changeover and on-site emergencies you will almost definitely need to employ an agent, cleaner or a caretaker to help look after your property.

Unfortunately, the very nature of holiday lettings can mean that it is a sporadic business, so it may not be as easy to employ someone on a casual basis. Whoever you employ, you will need to be confident of their standards and their reliability. You may need to think about a contingency plan in case of an illness or other personal situations. You need to be confident that they will be able to prepare the property if you get a sudden late booking, and be able to cope with an emergency.

A SECOND HOME

You may already have a second home or holiday home that you want to adapt to holiday lettings. As it is already furnished and equipped, it may appear to be a fairly simple transition. But switching over to holiday lettings is a very different business. You may already occasionally let your own 'holiday home' to friends and family and may have charged a little for this. You will probably not have employed a cleaner and more often than not your visitors will have cleaned up before they left. You will have probably carried out some general maintenance and a periodic spring clean.

Your friends and family may not mind some dust and non-matching crockery, or a bedroom that lacks bedside lights. Indeed, they will be grateful for the opportunity to use your second home. But for anyone paying to stay in a self-catering property, they will be expecting very different standards. So, what might have seemed a painless move into this market now presents a variety of challenges. Not only will you have to look at the management of the property, but possibly refurbishing and equipping it as well. What will have been acceptable to you, your family and friends, may not meet all the demands and standards for the holiday market.

You will also need to change your philosophy of thinking of the property as your holiday home, and adapt to it being a business but with your occasional use. This will require a great deal of commitment to change. If you choose to have an agency to manage the property, they may also put some restrictions on the times that you can use the property. It will no longer be acceptable to leave your personal belongings around the place and these will have to be locked away when it is being let.

What was your second *home,* may now become your second *property*.

CONVERTING OUTBUILDINGS

For a number of operators there is the option of converting redundant buildings into one or more holiday units. This is often the case with farms diversifying into the holiday market and it often provides the opportunity to create self-catering units of interest and character.

Converting a building, whether it is an old barn or stables, will involve planning consent and other legal requirements. It will also require a major financial investment, and effective market research will be needed to ensure the project is going to be financially viable and rewarding. However, starting from scratch also gives you an opportunity to specifically design holiday units for a target market. This can provide you with the flexibility to appeal to groups and families, yet still accommodate independent bookings. In addition, you can design units to specifically meet the needs of the accessible or disabled market, a sector that holds great potential.

Letting more than one unit will make greater demands on your time, especially on changeover day, and you may need to employ staff. The more units you have, the greater will be the need for help.

AN INVESTMENT PROPERTY

You may be considering purchasing a property as an investment or for your retirement. Apart from the purchase costs, this will involve fees for estate agents, solicitors and surveyors long before you start to equip and furnish the property. Unless you have the necessary funding, you will need to organise finance and in order to borrow money from a bank or building society, you will need to submit a business plan including an operating budget and cash flow forecast.

All banks offer help for people wanting to start a business and are worth approaching. Most will be able provide a 'Business start-up pack'. However, if you are thinking of buying a property, make sure you carefully consider its location and whether there is sufficient demand for self-catering in that area. You will also need to consider the management of the property, as discussed above, and should carry out some market research to determine visitor rates and seasonality.

What will it cost?

If you are sure that developing a self-catering property is the right decision for you, you need to be prepared to make a significant financial commitment and consider all the costs involved.

LIKELY COSTS FOR A SELF-CATERING PROPERTY

Unlike a B&B where you could possibly let just one room without too much investment, you will be letting a whole property. This will need to be furnished and equipped and you will be running a business with various associated costs. Visitor expectations are high, and where it might be tolerable for a guest to spend one night in a B&B with a small bedroom and a very compact bathroom, paying money to spend a week in a poorly laid out and furnished self-catering property is not acceptable.

The likely costs associated with operating a self-catering property can be broken down into various components. These are as follows:

INITIAL COSTS

If you are purchasing a property, or altering or converting an existing building, you will need to make planning applications or gain permission for change of use. You may need to employ a surveyor, an architect and possibly various builders. These costs will vary depending on the scale of the project, and you will need to manage your project costs carefully to optimise your business.

PREPARATION COSTS

The costs involved in getting a property prepared for holiday lets are varied, but will include amongst others: decorating, furnishing and equipping the property, gaining insurance for buildings, contents and public liability, advertising and marketing the property, and possibly membership of local tourism associations and tourist boards.

ANNUAL EXPENSES

Within the annual costs of operating your self-catering business will be quarterly expenses, including electricity and fuel (these will vary depending on occupancy), water rates and sewerage charges and possibly telephone line rentals.

Monthly costs may include business rates or council tax. These are often dependant on the number of days you let within the year, but it will be prudent to check with your local authority on the current rules for both.

Annual expenses will include appliance servicing, a chimney sweep if you have an open fire or a wood burner, insurances and possibly an accountant, and any relevant subscriptions.

ONGOING OPERATIONAL COSTS

As well as the costs detailed above there will be ongoing costs for laundry, cleaning materials, repairs and maintenance, replacement of damaged items, telephone, postage, stationery and, if you employ staff, wages. In addition, there may be the cost of a welcome pack, basic groceries or a gift that you provide for your guests, as well as potential further costs should the unexpected happen.

Additional costs may include agency fees, advertising and marketing. Finally, depending on the number of properties that you let and the income generated, you could be liable to VAT.

After taking all of these costs into account, you will hopefully be aiming to maximise occupancy and achieve a good return on your investment.

Next chapter

The next chapter looks at how you should plan the development of your self-catering property. It identifies aspects of the letting market you should be aware of and discusses how to set your prices, who your guests are likely to be and some legal aspects you should be aware of.

Chapter 2
Planning

Having decided that operating a self-catering property is the right decision for you, what should you do next? In this chapter we focus on the market research you should carry out to understand the tourism industry and the self-catering industry where you are. We look at the various types of markets that exist and the needs of different types of guests. This will help you to identify the market in your area and highlight what type of guest you may want to attract to your property. We also look at the different factors you should consider when setting your rates and the importance of managing your booking season. Towards the end of the chapter we look at various legal considerations you may need to take into account before, and whilst, operating your property.

Identifying your market

The location of your property may determine the type of guest who will want to stay, and might also affect how you furnish and equip the property. Identifying the precise market you want to attract or may be in a position to attract will also determine how and where you promote and advertise your property.

WHO STAYS IN SELF-CATERING?
When people think of tourists they often think of holidaymakers. Our impression of the tourist is often fixed on this image. However, when the tourist board think of tourists they think of anyone away from their

home. And when you consider who may be travelling away from home, for whatever reason, the definition of a tourist becomes very wide indeed. So who does stay away from home, and who is looking for a self-catering property to stay in?

Broadly speaking, guests fall into one of two categories: those away for leisure, and those away for work and relocation, but within these two categories there are many reasons why people stay away from home. They may be on holiday or having a long weekend away. They may be working in the area, moving job and about to move home. There are very many reasons why people stay away and all will have different requirements, wherever they stay. We look at the needs of different guests in Chapters 5, 6 and 7.

THE DIFFERENT MARKETS

The markets for the self-catering industry are numerous and can be divided into many diverse categories. Here we will focus on typical family groupings, including couples, families and groups, and the reasons for guests to stay, including the business market, guests with pets, overseas visitors, activity breaks and the weekend market, to help you understand the self-catering industry. Within each of these markets there will be different requirements and expectations. It is by exceeding these expectations that you can create a successful business, and by offering distinctiveness you can encourage repeat, recommended and referral business.

COUPLES

Couples may be working professionals who take regular breaks to 'recharge their batteries'. They may be used to high-quality standards in their own home, and on holiday may be expecting a wide range of facilities and high levels of quality in both furnishings and equipment. Expectations may include the provision of CD/DVD players and flatscreen TVs, and in the kitchen, high-quality equipment and pots and pans, even though they may do little or no cooking. Indeed, they may even look for a property that can offer a home-catering service.

Although most lettings will be weekly, in the off or shoulder seasons (early spring and late autumn) this market may be attracted to short breaks, whether midweek or weekend.

RETIRED COUPLES

The more mature market may be retired and may have more time and money to take additional holidays within the year. Like the couples market, they may also expect high standards and may appreciate some additional comforts, such as a walk-in shower, chairs that are easy to get in and out of, and additional heating.

As with couples, this market can also be attracted to short breaks in both the off and shoulder seasons.

FAMILIES

Families may be with young children, but may also include grandparents. The market may also include family and friends, and could contain two or three groups coming in separate cars and from different locations to holiday together. Their expectations may be for plenty of space, a large kitchen and dining area, more than one bathroom (with at least one fitted with a bath as opposed to a shower for babies and younger children), cots, highchairs and stairgates. They may also want a secure garden, nearby child-friendly activities, games and a close location to eateries.

Another section within this market will be family celebrations for birthdays or anniversaries. They will require plenty of kitchen equipment and crockery, and could benefit from staying in multi-unit properties.

GROUPS

Groups may mean a number of couples together, a family or friends' reunion or a sporting break, perhaps for golf. They will probably expect more than one bathroom and will appreciate plenty of comfortably furnished seating areas. This market can also include hen and stag parties, which can be quite demanding. You may decide that single gender groups are not the market that you want to attract. However, if this is a market that does appeal to you, your guests may be interested in information on local entertainment and socialising venues, and less interested in dining and kitchen arrangements.

BUSINESS MARKET

It is becoming more normal now for people to work away from home for a number of days a week and many may prefer the opportunity to rent a holiday property instead of staying in a hotel or a B&B. By staying in a self-catering property, the business market will have more privacy and usually be able to relax more. They will want home comforts, plenty of space to work in and plenty of socket points with good heating and lighting arrangements.

It is not unusual for touring theatre groups to rent holiday homes whilst performing in an area as, due to their working schedule, staying in a hotel can be disturbing when they want to sleep during the day. Such groups may be attracted to larger properties with more than one bathroom and will want plenty of space for storing costumes and rehearsing.

PET OWNERS

The number of properties willing to take pets is limited, so targeting pet owners could potentially be a good business move.

Your location would need to be somewhere that provides good walking areas, and whilst you may not be expected to provide high-quality furnishings, an enclosed safe garden would be a priority. If you have a shared garden, you may need to specify a certain part of the garden for pets' use, and perhaps provide a dedicated litterbin for waste.

The downside to taking pets will be that there is nearly always extra cleaning required. There can be damage to paintwork and not all pet owners will keep their dogs off furnishings and bedding. You will also need to consider that other visitors who will use the property may be allergic to pets and be aware, in some instances, that pet smells can linger.

OVERSEAS VISITORS

The overseas market will usually travel lighter than the domestic market and so will almost always require bed linen and towelling to be included within the hire of the holiday home. This market is often interested in places to visit and things to do, and so may want to be near to visitor attractions, such as museums and galleries, but also close to the open countryside and heritage sites. Where you are located will often determine what you should provide for this market, but ample guidebooks, leaflets, maps and information will be important.

OUTDOOR MARKET

The outdoor activity market can include many types of visitors of any age, and will include walkers, cyclists, birdwatchers and guests on fishing holidays. The outdoor market will tend to spend most of the day away from the property, pursuing their interest, and they will probably not expect or need the highest level of quality in furnishings and decoration. However, they will probably need safe storage for any equipment, such as bicycles or fishing rods, and may appreciate good washing, drying and airing facilities for outdoor clothing. In addition, they may need plenty of comprehensive local information and maps.

LUXURY WEEKENDS

Guests away on a luxury break will be expecting an excellent level of quality in every aspect of the accommodation, from furnishings and lighting, to bathrooms and bedding. In addition, they will probably expect a wide range of accessories, including high-quality televisions and audio equipment. By adding a good quality welcome pack and providing information on restaurants and entertainment, you can help meet and exceed the needs of this market.

ACCESSIBLE MARKET

The requirements of the Disability Discrimination Act are covered in more detail later in this chapter, but the act requires you to take reasonable steps to make your accommodation accessible to a guest with a disability. It is worth noting here that the accessible market is a growth market and it does not only cover visitors who lack mobility but can also apply to someone who is visually impaired, hard of hearing or has learning difficulties. For more detailed advice on meeting the needs of the accessible market you should obtain details on VisitBritain's National Accessible Scheme from Quality in Tourism (see details in sources of further help at the end of this book).

IDENTIFYING TRENDS

With all of the above types of visitors come trends in the letting year. Letting trends are not always consistent. There are peaks and troughs. In Chapter 9 we will look at how to grow your business and how to identify the peaks and troughs in the letting year. But be aware that for most self-catering operators, there will be peak months and very quiet periods.

A typical year may be a relatively quiet winter with a busy summer, but this does over-simplify the picture. Within the year there will always be opportunities to pick up business. You may be located in a city centre with year-round business, or near to a theatre with Christmas pantomimes. You may decide to hold out for weekly lets in the summer (the peak season) and at high-demand times (Christmas and New Year), but consider short breaks in the early spring and late autumn (the shoulder season). It is a good idea to map out the year by identifying events and high-demand periods (such as Easter and school holidays). This can be a very useful way of predicting when you should be busy and becomes an invaluable tool when it comes to knowing how to let your accommodation. For example, it may help you to decide whether you should take a weekend booking when you know the holiday season is just starting and you should be able to let the property for a full week.

Researching the market

Researching the market will help highlight how busy the area is, what level of quality is being offered and what rates other self-catering properties are charging.

STEP 1 – GATHER BROCHURES AND INFORMATION FROM OTHER OPERATORS

A very good first step for anyone considering starting self-catering is to research the competition by obtaining their brochures and tariff charges. Part of this can be done by using the Internet and the VisitBritain website or local accommodation guides that cover the area. Different tariffs will reflect different-sized properties as well as the different range of facilities available, such as en-suite rooms, swimming pools and games rooms, and the different standards of quality they offer.

STEP 2 – CONTACT YOUR TOURIST INFORMATION CENTRE

To get the best idea of what tariffs are being charged in your area and to obtain an objective point of view you could contact your local Tourist (also known as Visitor) Information Centre (TIC) for help and advice. The staff in the information centre deal with up to 1,000 enquiries a day, both face to face and over the telephone. In addition, they respond to e-mails, distribute tens of thousands of accommodation guides and meet the needs of thousands of people using the Internet to find accommodation. In many TICs, the staff make accommodation bookings on a daily basis and quickly build up a very clear idea of how busy a particular area is. Whilst bookings for self-catering lets do not feature on a large scale in TICs away from the busiest holiday areas, staff can nevertheless provide you with excellent advice on peaks and troughs within the year and the events that can generate high demand for accommodation. The TIC may also be able to provide information on any future local developments that may bring in additional demand for accommodation.

In addition, the TIC can provide you with a local accommodation guide. This guide will be a very useful place to start your research. It will contain a listing of the self-catering properties in your area and can often tell you how large they are, what they charge and where they are located. From this information you will be able to see how you fit into the overall picture and start to get an idea of what you will be able to charge for your property.

STEP 3 – CONTACT OTHER SELF-CATERING PROPERTIES

The other self-catering operators in your area may at first appear as competitors. After all, you are all competing for the same market. But consider this again. If a nearby self-catering property is full and receives an enquiry, who could they pass the business on to? If you have a good relationship with your neighbouring self-catering properties, then you may quickly

---

Identifying your market

- WHO STAYS IN SELF-CATERING?
- THE DIFFERENT MARKETS
- COUPLES
- RETIRED COUPLES
- FAMILIES
- GROUPS
- BUSINESS MARKET
- PET OWNERS
- OVERSEAS VISITORS
- OUTDOOR MARKET
- LUXURY WEEKENDS
- ACCESSIBLE MARKET
- IDENTIFYING TRENDS

Researching the market

- STEP 1 – GATHER BROCHURES AND INFORMATION FROM OTHER OPERATORS
- STEP 2 – CONTACT YOUR LOCAL TOURIST INFORMATION CENTRE
- STEP 3 – CONTACT OTHER SELF-CATERING PROPERTIES

reap the benefits of referral business. Of course, an operator will always try and sell an alternative set of dates first, but where there is no movement by the prospective customer, referral can be a useful tool.

Most importantly, you should also consider joining a local accommodation group. Many exist throughout the country, whether they are national groups or local. Groups are a very helpful resource for comparing notes, learning from other operators who may be much more experienced than yourself, and for sharing business.

Case study

Working together – an example of an accommodation group

The Bedfordshire & Hertfordshire Farm & Country Accommodation Group is a very good example of an industry grouping that acts as a kind of co-operative. It does not set out to have fiercely commercial aims for itself, but to provide a support mechanism for its members. It started some 21 years ago with three members and now has about 25 small operators, covering B&Bs and self-catering properties. It uses subscriptions from its membership to add strength to their limited marketing activity. This has included the production of a group brochure promoted through each other, local TICs and businesses, at leaflet swap-shops in conjunction with visitor attractions, and at various shows and events. Enterprisingly, their latest venture is to redesign the group website as it has been recognised that this is an increasingly important portal for enquiries and bookings. A new feature will be to create more hyperlinks, in and out, particularly useful for potential customers visiting a nearby attraction website in relation to a weekend event.

The greatest advantage of the group, however, is the referral aspect that it brings. Small self-catering properties in a busy area with a lot of business tourism

---

are often booked up and it is an extended service to the customer, and each other, that bookings can be referred on to another group member with confidence. The group all know, or know of, each other very well through a modest but vibrant social programme that helps to provide added cohesiveness. All of the group members are quality assured.

Researching the market

- STEP 1 — GATHER BROCHURES AND INFORMATION FROM OTHER OPERATORS

- STEP 2 — CONTACT YOUR LOCAL TOURIST INFORMATION CENTRE

- STEP 3 — CONTACT OTHER SELF-CATERING PROPERTIES

Assess your property

Assess your property

- HOW MANY GUESTS SHOULD YOU ACCOMMODATE?

- SOFA BEDS

- MULTIPLE UNITS

Having an idea of the market that is attracted to your area, or which you may want to target, will influence how you develop your property and the style of furniture and type of décor you decide on. One of the first questions you need to ask yourself is how many guests you can accommodate comfortably. This will depend on the size of the rooms when they are fully furnished and possibly the number of bathrooms you will be able to provide. Visitor expectations for holiday accommodation are increasing as they experience higher standards in the UK and overseas.

HOW MANY GUESTS SHOULD YOU ACCOMMODATE?
It can be tempting to maximise the number of bed spaces in your property in the belief it will maximise bookings. This is not the case.

Consider a two-bedroom property. A good set-up would be to have a double-bedded room and a twin-bedded room. This will provide you with a reasonable degree of flexibility, allowing the accommodation to be let to a single person, a couple, three friends or a small family. If there is sufficient space in one of the bedrooms, this could accommodate a travel cot. Trying to put more beds into the property, even if space allows, will affect the rest of your property and how it is used.

Bunk beds are quite common in self-catering properties and you could consider placing bunk beds into a smaller room, which would appeal to young children. However, if there is only one other bedroom, you may find that this restricts your bookings, as it is unlikely this room would appeal to adults.

With more than two bedrooms you can more easily meet the needs of the family and group market. But, be careful. However many guests you accommodate, you need sufficient space elsewhere in the property to ensure your guests are comfortable. And you need sufficient bathrooms and WCs. Lacking enough toilet facilities could cause inconvenience, and lacking space may prevent your guests sitting together in the living and dining rooms.

SOFA BEDS

Think carefully about the number of guests that you can comfortably accommodate. Sofa beds can be used to provide supplementary sleeping and greater flexibility, but the lack of privacy they bring means they are perhaps more suited for the occasional visitor. Not all adults would welcome spending a week on a sofa bed in the sitting room. So, if you have a two-bedroom property that has a double and twin bedroom plus a sofa bed in the sitting room, you would need to advertise it accordingly as 'Sleeps 4 (+2)'. Take into account that anyone sleeping on a sofa bed will still need somewhere to keep clothing and you will also need appropriate storage for bedding when it is not in use.

MULTIPLE UNITS

If you are converting redundant buildings you may have the potential to construct a number of units. This will give you greater flexibility in creating a variety of units to accommodate different sized groups. You may be able to create a studio apartment, or one-bedroom, two-bedroom or three-bedroom units. You may create interconnecting units for larger groups or you may develop all units identically, allowing you to let the space out as suits you best.

Multi units can be very popular and might appear to be financially rewarding, but bear in mind that holiday visitors require plenty of comfortable space and adequate privacy. If developing a multi-unit property, try to create privacy for each unit. Consider having effective screening between the units, dedicated patios and individual parking bays, rather than just one shared garden with shared furniture.

Setting your rates

In Chapter 1 we looked at the likely costs you will incur in operating a self-catering property, and earlier in this chapter we looked at three suggested steps you should take to research and understand your market. You should now be ready to consider what rates to set for your letting tariff.

THE COMPETITION

Firstly, consider the competition in your area. By now you will have done some research and will know how much others are charging. You will see the rates they charge for peak season, shoulder season and the off season. In addition, you have seen what size their property is, how many guests they can accommodate, what facilities are provided and, if graded, what the quality rating is. You may even notice that the higher the quality rating, the more the self-catering property charges. This may not always be the case, but it often goes hand in hand that the higher the quality, the higher the price. That said, some operators that achieve a higher rating keep their prices very competitive and use the pulling power of the higher rating.

When setting your rates, it can often be a good idea to ensure your rates are not vastly different from the competition. This may not always be the case. You may be in a situation where you are offering exceptional quality and want to charge a rate to reflect that. This may put you into a very different price category to other holiday homes in your area, but that will need to be a business decision you make. Similarly, if you are situated in a 'honey pot' location you can possibly aim for a higher rate. But generally, it is going to be the local market, your competitors and their rates that ultimately dictate how much you can charge.

YOUR FACILITIES

When setting your rates, take into account what other properties are offering, so you can make a fair comparison with your own property. Consider what facilities they offer and what facilities you can offer. For example, do they offer en-suite accommodation, private gardens and games rooms? Do they include electricity and heating, logs, linen and towels?

If you have a multi-unit property, then as well as setting rates relative to other self-catering properties, you may also decide to charge different rates for each unit, based on overall space and general appointment.

YOUR PROFIT MARGIN

Once you have an idea of your tariff, you can estimate your predicted income based on your expected occupancy throughout the year. Offset this against the likely costs of running the property for a year (see Chapter 1). Does this give you a sufficient profit?

Managing your bookings

A further consideration when planning your business and setting your rates is how you are going to manage your bookings. Do you intend to let your property for the full year or for only part of the year, taking into account your liability for council tax or business rates? Are you planning to take bookings for short breaks of three nights or will you only let for a full week?

SEASONAL VARIATIONS

The high season for holidaymakers in the UK is during the main school holiday in July, August and early September, as well as at Christmas and the New Year. High occupancy will also come during other periods in the year, such as at Easter and school half-term holidays. Demand can extend into the shoulder season in the spring and autumn. If you intend to have your property available over the winter period, potential occupancy levels may be lower, but your operational costs for electricity and fuel will be higher. As a result, arriving at realistic rates that are competitive whilst covering your costs and producing a profit can be complicated.

SHORT BREAKS

Many people now want to take short breaks or go away for a long weekend. As this is a growth market you will need to assess the pros and cons of meeting this demand.

Taking a three-night stay may actually make inroads into two weeks, as Friday is often the day when guests want to start their weekend break. In effect, you could have lost the potential of two full weeks, occupancy whilst taking a three-night break, so you may want to have a higher 'daily' rate for the short break market.

WINTER LETS

You may have decided to let only for the main season of Easter to October, but there is another way of extending your season. Many owners make their properties available for a short-term let during the winter season.

There are naturally pros and cons. If you are successful in obtaining a short-term tenant, you may need to have a formal contract drawn up. The rent would have to take into account fuel, electricity and wear and tear. The downside (and there usually is one) is that you can never guarantee how careful the tenant will be. There may be additional damages or it may be difficult to get them to leave in time for you to prepare for the coming season. It would also be prudent to check that you would not be breaching any regulations for council tax purposes.

However, it can often work very well. Your insurance company will probably be pleased that the property is not left unoccupied. The extra rent can also be useful for offsetting your costs of maintenance, replacements, decoration and advertising.

Legal considerations

You may already have an idea as to where your target market is likely to come from and want to tailor your property accordingly to meet this market. But before you start knocking down walls and buying the furniture, you will need to be aware of legislation.

This next section concentrates on the various laws which may affect you when operating your self-catering property. It is only intended as general guidance and is not definitive legal advice. It is designed to raise awareness of the pertinent issues that need to be considered. For more detailed advice on legal considerations for self-catering properties, please

Setting your rates
- THE COMPETITION
- YOUR FACILITIES
- YOUR PROFIT MARGIN

Managing your bookings
- SEASONAL VARIATIONS
- SHORT BREAKS
- WINTER LETS

Legal considerations
- PLANNING PERMISSION AND BUILDING REGULATIONS
- BUSINESS RATES
- LETTING OPTIONS FOR SELF-CATERING ACCOMMODATION
- PRIVATE WATER SUPPLIES
- THE RESALE OF GAS AND ELECTRICITY
- HEALTH AND SAFETY
- INSTALLING AND MAINTAINING GAS APPLIANCES
- ELECTRICAL EQUIPMENT
- GENERAL PRODUCT SAFETY
- FIRE SAFETY OF FURNITURE IN SELF-CATERING ACCOMMODATION
- TELEVISION LICENCES
- THE TRADE DESCRIPTIONS ACT 1968
- THE DISABILITY DISCRIMINATION ACT

consult the Pink Booklet. This is a guide to legislation and other regulations that affect accommodation businesses, and is available from VisitBritain whose contact details will be found in Sources of futher help.

The following text is an adaptation of some of the information to be found in the Pink Booklet. The areas covered here are not exhaustive, but cover the main issues of:

- Planning permission and building regulations
- Business rates
- Letting options for self-catering accommodation
- Private water supplies
- The resale of gas and electricity
- Health and safety
- Installing and maintaining gas appliances
- Electrical equipment
- General product safety
- Fire safety of furniture in self-catering accommodation
- Television licences
- Trade Descriptions Act
- The Disability Discrimination Act

PLANNING PERMISSION AND BUILDING REGULATIONS
Essential first steps

Planning permission and building regulations are the essential first steps if you are considering offering self-catering accommodation.

Planning permission

If you are considering:

- starting a new business, or
- converting or extending your premises,

you should contact the planning department of your local authority for their advice on planning permission at a very early stage.

Even if you only wish to equip an existing building as a holiday cottage, where no structural alterations to the property will be carried out, you may need 'change of use' planning permission to do so.

Local authorities' policies on granting planning permission vary – the effects on neighbours, car parking facilities and the number of bedrooms offered for letting are all issues that an authority may take into consideration when deciding whether planning permission is necessary or when considering an application.

Building regulations

Structural alterations to a property or the construction of a new building will also be subject to building regulations.

BUSINESS RATES

Unless you do not intend your property to be available for short lets for 140 days or more a year, you will need to pay business rates. These are calculated on your property's 'Rateable Value', which is based on the rental value of your property. These values are set by an independent government agency, the Valuation Office.

You can obtain details of the Rateable Value of your property from your local Valuation Office or the business rates department of your local authority.

LETTING OPTIONS FOR SELF-CATERING ACCOMMODATION

Holiday letting

If you let a property for holiday purposes, the law allows you to do this without your guests gaining any rights to stay on in the property. There is no limit to the length of the holiday let, but it must actually be for a holiday.

As a matter of good practice, you are recommended to have a basic agreement with your guests (this can be by letter) which includes a statement that you are letting the premises as a holiday let, with the start and end days of the let clearly stated.

Out-of-season letting

If you are thinking of supplementing your income by letting your property for a number of months out of season, you can opt for either (a) an assured tenancy or (b) an assured shorthold tenancy. More details on both can be found in the Pink Booklet.

Legal considerations
- PLANNING PERMISSION AND BUILDING REGULATIONS
- BUSINESS RATES
- LETTING OPTIONS FOR SELF-CATERING ACCOMMODATION
- PRIVATE WATER SUPPLIES
- THE RESALE OF GAS AND ELECTRICITY
- HEALTH AND SAFETY
- INSTALLING AND MAINTAINING GAS APPLIANCES
- ELECTRICAL EQUIPMENT
- GENERAL PRODUCT SAFETY
- FIRE SAFETY OF FURNITURE IN SELF-CATERING ACCOMMODATION
- TELEVISION LICENCES
- THE TRADE DESCRIPTIONS ACT 1968
- THE DISABILITY DISCRIMINATION ACT

PRIVATE WATER SUPPLIES

Private water supplies include water from springs, streams, boreholes or wells. These supplies are currently regulated by the Private Water Supplies Regulations 1991 to provide a reasonable measure of protection to consumers of water from private supplies.

Do these regulations affect me?

- **Yes** – if the water supplies for your self-catering establishment come from a private supply.

Private water supply tests

Local authorities are required to test nearly all private water supplies. Current sampling frequencies range from less than once a year for the smallest supplies to as often as 24 times a year for much larger ones.

THE RESALE OF GAS AND ELECTRICITY

If you are reselling gas and/or electricity that has already been bought from an authorised supplier, the most you can charge is limited by the 'maximum resale price rule'.

Do maximum resale prices apply to me?

- **Yes** – if you make a specific charge to your customers for gas or electricity, whether or not you use individual meters to record their consumption.

The rule typically applies to self-catering accommodation, although it affects all forms of accommodation where separate charging occurs.

If you overcharge for electricity or gas, your customer can ask for a refund of the excess and can pursue the matter in the civil courts if necessary.

- **No** – if you do not make a specific charge for electricity and/or gas (e.g. if customers are charged a single rental figure for fully inclusive accommodation).

What is the current maximum resale price?

The maximum resale price is the same price that you have paid to your own supplier – put another way, you can only sell gas or electricity to your guests on a non-profit basis.

Price of energy units

If you are charged a single *unit* rate for gas or electricity by your own supplier, you must charge your customers the same rate. If the unit rate varies (e.g. because you pay on an Economy 7-type tariff, or prices vary on a seasonal basis), you will need to calculate an average price for each unit used.

HEALTH AND SAFETY

Your liability to guests and the public

Under the Occupiers' Liability Acts 1957 and 1984, the person who controls a premises (the 'occupier') is liable for the physical safety of everyone who comes onto the premises.

Occupiers have what is known as a 'duty of care' to guests and other visitors, and must make sure that the premises are reasonably safe for the purpose for which guests were invited to use them.

Does this legislation apply to me?

Yes – if you are the owner of a self-catering accommodation with control over your premises.

What does this mean in practice?

You must make sure that the premises are 'reasonably safe'. For example, you should ensure that floors are not slippery, passageways are clear, cables are tucked away, furniture and wall fixtures are secure, and that guests have been acquainted with emergency procedures and the layout of the premises, as appropriate.

If you have children staying on the premises, you need to make sure the premises are reasonably safe for them, not just adults.

Your duty of care does not normally extend to parts of your premises that are clearly marked as being out of bounds to guests.

Generally, the owner is also liable for accidents caused as a result of the actions of his or her staff or other guests. For example, if a member of staff leaves a bucket on the stairs and someone trips over it and injures themselves, you may be held responsible.

Legal considerations

- PLANNING PERMISSION AND BUILDING REGULATIONS
- BUSINESS RATES
- LETTING OPTIONS FOR SELF-CATERING ACCOMMODATION
- PRIVATE WATER SUPPLIES
- THE RESALE OF GAS AND ELECTRICITY
- HEALTH AND SAFETY
- INSTALLING AND MAINTAINING GAS APPLIANCES
- ELECTRICAL EQUIPMENT
- GENERAL PRODUCT SAFETY
- FIRE SAFETY OF FURNITURE IN SELF-CATERING ACCOMMODATION
- TELEVISION LICENCES
- THE TRADE DESCRIPTIONS ACT 1968
- THE DISABILITY DISCRIMINATION ACT

No matter how many notices you put up to the contrary and whatever your booking conditions may say, the law does not allow you to exclude or restrict your liability for death and injuries to guests arising from your negligence (or that of your staff or agents). However, you can take out insurance to cover your liability (see 'Insurance' below).

You will not though normally be liable for a guest who injures themselves whilst involved in an activity which is not something a guest might reasonably have been expected to do on the premises, such as abseiling from an upper floor window! Each guest has a duty to take care of his or her own safety. If his or her own negligence leads to an accident, this would reduce, or could even override, any liability that the owner would otherwise have had.

If anyone makes a claim against you, you should seek legal advice immediately.

Your liability to employees

Under the Employers' Liability (Compulsory Insurance) Act 1969, every employer must have insurance to cover their liability for any bodily injury or disease sustained by an employee at work. Failure to do this is a criminal offence.

How does this apply to you?

If you are a self-catering accommodation provider and you employ at least one person, you are required to take out and maintain employers' liability insurance cover with a minimum of £5 million for any one claim (most policies available offer £10 million cover).

You must display a copy of the certificate of insurance at your place(s) of business so that it can be seen and read by all your employees. The policy document, or a copy of it, must also be kept available for inspection by Health and Safety Executive inspectors and, for future reference, all policy documents should be retained permanently.

Have you adequate insurance cover?

If you start offering self-catering accommodation, you need to consider whether you have adequate insurance to cover, for example, your potential liability under the Occupiers' and

Employers' Liability Acts. Most household policies will not cover (i) your use of the premises for business purposes, (ii) your legal liability to employees or paying guests, or (iii) any theft or damage to your property by guests. In any event, you should contact your existing insurers as soon as possible.

Public liability insurance

One type of insurance cover you should consider, particularly as the public becomes increasingly claims conscious, is public liability insurance. This covers your liability to guests and others for injury, loss and damage (for example, under the Occupiers' Liability Acts).

There is no legal requirement to take out public liability insurance, but it is a requirement for participation in the VisitBritain Self-Catering Accommodation Quality Assurance scheme.

Other types of insurance

Public liability insurance must not be confused with the employers' liability insurance. It also does not cover loss or damage to the proprietors' property.

INSTALLING AND MAINTAINING GAS APPLIANCES

Each year there are proven complaints from guests about the safety of gas appliances in their accommodation premises, normally self-catering. The Gas Safety (Installation and Use) Regulations 1998 are there to protect you and your guests.

What do the regulations cover?

- The regulations specifically deal with the installation, maintenance and use of gas appliances, fittings and flues in domestic, residential and commercial premises.
- The regulations place duties on a wide range of people including gas suppliers and those installing and working on gas equipment.
- The regulations include extensive duties on landlords for ensuring appliances and flues in the premises they let are safely maintained and checked.

What types of premises are affected?

The premises affected include all domestic, residential and sleeping accommodation, including self-catering properties.

Legal considerations

- PLANNING PERMISSION AND BUILDING REGULATIONS
- BUSINESS RATES
- LETTING OPTIONS FOR SELF-CATERING ACCOMMODATION
- PRIVATE WATER SUPPLIES
- THE RESALE OF GAS AND ELECTRICITY
- HEALTH AND SAFETY
- INSTALLING AND MAINTAINING GAS APPLIANCES
- ELECTRICAL EQUIPMENT
- GENERAL PRODUCT SAFETY
- FIRE SAFETY OF FURNITURE IN SELF-CATERING ACCOMMODATION
- TELEVISION LICENCES
- THE TRADE DESCRIPTIONS ACT 1968
- THE DISABILITY DISCRIMINATION ACT

What are my main duties?

(a) As a landlord (and for the purposes of these regulations, 'landlords' includes owners of self-catering accommodation), you are required to:

- ensure all gas fittings and flues are maintained in a safe condition
- ensure an annual safety check is carried out on each gas appliance/flue (all safety checks must be carried out by a CORGI registered fitter)
- keep a written record of the inspection for two years (containing the information such as the date of the check, location and details of the appliance/flue, any defects found and action taken, and confirming that the check was made in accordance with the regulations. CORGI has devised checklists that may be used for this purpose)
- issue a copy of the record to each new tenant staying for more than 28 days, or if the premises is let for 28 days or less, display a copy of the record prominently in the premises.

(b) As an employer: if you are an employer you have a duty to ensure that the gas appliances under your control are 'maintained in a safe condition so as to prevent injury to any person'.

Your liability and your agent's

If you use an agent to manage your property, you should ensure that the management contract specifies who is responsible for the maintenance of gas appliances and for keeping records to indicate when this maintenance has been carried out.

The liability of purely marketing and booking agencies (rather than managing agencies) under these regulations is unclear. Some agencies are therefore seeking to exclude themselves from liability by inserting into their contracts with owners a clause which commits those owners to ensuring that their property complies at all times with the gas safety requirements.

ELECTRICAL EQUIPMENT

What do the regulations cover?

The Electrical Equipment (Safety) Regulations 1994 require, amongst other things, that all electrical equipment supplied 'in the course of business' is safe. This applies equally to new and second-hand equipment.

Do the regulations apply to me?

The regulations apply to everyone who supplies electrical equipment in the course of their business, regardless of whether or not their business is actually the supply of electrical equipment. The regulations are particularly relevant to self-catering accommodation.

What does 'safe' mean?

For electrical equipment to be regarded as safe, there should be no risk (or only a minimal risk) that the equipment will in any way cause death or injury to any person or domestic animal, or cause damage to property.

Nowadays if you are buying any new electrical equipment in the UK it should be 'safe', as manufacturers and suppliers are bound by the same regulations. It should also carry a CE marking (indicating that the manufacturer believes the product complies with all relevant European safety standards). If you are buying second-hand electrical equipment from a professional dealer (or auction house) it should likewise be 'safe', although it does not have to carry a CE marking.

Do I need to maintain electrical equipment?

Although these regulations require electrical equipment to be safe, they make no specific provisions for maintenance. However, to be sure that the electrical equipment in your accommodation remains safe, you are strongly advised to have it checked and serviced regularly.

Letting agents can also be held responsible for the safety of the electrical equipment in accommodation they let, depending on the terms of their agreements with property owners.

Legal considerations

- PLANNING PERMISSION AND BUILDING REGULATIONS
- BUSINESS RATES
- LETTING OPTIONS FOR SELF-CATERING ACCOMMODATION
- PRIVATE WATER SUPPLIES
- THE RESALE OF GAS AND ELECTRICITY
- HEALTH AND SAFETY
- INSTALLING AND MAINTAINING GAS APPLIANCES
- ELECTRICAL EQUIPMENT
- GENERAL PRODUCT SAFETY
- FIRE SAFETY OF FURNITURE IN SELF-CATERING ACCOMMODATION
- TELEVISION LICENCES
- THE TRADE DESCRIPTIONS ACT 1968
- THE DISABILITY DISCRIMINATION ACT

GENERAL PRODUCT SAFETY

Do the regulations apply to me?

- **Yes** – if you are providing self-catering accommodation.

What do the current regulations cover?

The General Product Safety Regulations 1994 are aimed at making sure that certain goods supplied to consumers (new or second-hand) are safe. The regulations include consumer goods provided as part of self-catering holiday accommodation. The regulations only cover consumer goods not already covered by other pieces of safety regulation, for example, household goods but not electrical goods, or upholstered furniture.

How do I comply with the regulations?

The essential requirement is to ensure that you supply only safe products to your guests. A safe product is defined as one which 'under normal or reasonably foreseeable conditions of use, including duration, presents no risk or only the minimum risk compatible with the product's use and which is consistent with a high level of protection for consumers'.

Your guests will often be aware, through their own general knowledge and experience, of the potential risks of misusing products. However, this does not rule out the need for you, as the owner or letting agent, to take precautions in order to make sure, as far as you can, that the 'products' you supply are safe. This is not as daunting as it sounds. For example:

- if instructions are needed to operate a piece of household equipment, make sure that they are provided
- if an ironing board is likely to collapse because the legs are loose or fragile, repair it
- if an item of furniture or equipment can be damaged and made dangerous by children playing with it, make sure your guests know this.

You can no doubt think of your own examples and the best way to deal with them. The regulations require no formal testing or precautionary requirements and as you can see from the examples we have given, it is really just a matter of common sense and routine checking.

This said, it is important to note that there some specific requirements in relation to certain items of furniture. The Bunk Beds (Entrapment Hazards) (Safety) Regulations 1987 specify, for example, that 'a bunk bed should be constructed as to prevent any possibility of any part of the body of a child under six years old becoming wedged or trapped in any part of the bed's structure'. If you are uncertain about whether or not any item of your furniture meets the national safety requirements it is always best to seek professional legal advice.

Letting agents can be held responsible for product safety in the accommodation, depending on the terms of their agreement with the property owners.

FIRE SAFETY OF FURNITURE IN SELF-CATERING ACCOMMODATION

Do the regulations apply to me?
- **Yes** – if you are providing self-catering accommodation that contains upholstered furniture.

What do the regulations cover?
The Furniture and Furnishings (Fire) (Safety) Regulations 1988 (as amended) set fire resistance standards for upholstered furniture in domestic use (new and second-hand).

The regulations apply only to upholstered furniture supplied for domestic use, a type of use that implies a low fire hazard. Most holiday lets are regarded as constituting domestic use and, therefore, are covered by the regulations.

Furniture designed to cope with a greater fire hazard is available and may be offered to you by some retailers. When re-equipping your self-catering property, it will normally be for you to decide whether or not you require the new furniture to meet these higher fire resistance standards. If in any doubt, check with your local fire authority.

What furniture is affected?
Furniture must be upholstered to come within the scope of the regulations. Such furniture would include:

Legal considerations

- PLANNING PERMISSION AND BUILDING REGULATIONS
- BUSINESS RATES
- LETTING OPTIONS FOR SELF-CATERING ACCOMMODATION
- PRIVATE WATER SUPPLIES
- THE RESALE OF GAS AND ELECTRICITY
- HEALTH AND SAFETY
- INSTALLING AND MAINTAINING GAS APPLIANCES
- ELECTRICAL EQUIPMENT
- GENERAL PRODUCT SAFETY
- FIRE SAFETY OF FURNITURE IN SELF-CATERING ACCOMMODATION
- TELEVISION LICENCES
- THE TRADE DESCRIPTIONS ACT 1968
- THE DISABILITY DISCRIMINATION ACT

- domestic furniture, including children's furniture
- beds and divans (including their bases and headboards), mattresses of any size
- sofa beds, futons and other convertibles
- nursery furniture (e.g. highchairs, cots and playpens)
- domestic garden furniture
- scatter cushions and seat pads
- pillows.

The regulations also cover loose and stretch covers for furniture.

What furniture is not affected?

The regulations do *not* apply to:

- bedclothes (including duvets)
- loose covers for mattresses
- pillowcases
- curtains
- carpets
- sleeping bags
- goods made before 1 January 1950 and the materials used to re-upholster them.

Main provisions of the regulations

All furniture (new and second-hand) in your self-catering accommodation that is covered by the regulations must comply with certain safety tests.

All new upholstered furniture (except mattresses and bedding) and loose and stretch covers for furniture must carry a permanent label detailing compliance with fire safety requirements. Always look for these labels before buying any upholstered furniture for your property.

If you are having items reupholstered, make sure that the materials used comply with the regulations. Remember, however, that the regulations do not apply to materials used to reupholster furniture made before 1950, unless that furniture is being significantly reworked and upholstered.

Are letting agencies caught by the regulations?
Possibly. Whether or not an agency is liable for the fire safety of the furniture in the properties it handles will depend, the DTI believes, on the terms of its arrangement with you, the owner of the accommodation.

It seems that agencies that do no more than market your property and take bookings are unlikely to be liable. Nevertheless, as this is something of a grey area, some marketing/booking agencies cover themselves by including in their contracts with owners a clause which commits those owners to ensuring that their property complies at all times with these regulations (and others).

Agencies that also manage and maintain properties on an owner's behalf could possibly be liable.

Expect any prospective agency to ask about the fire resistance standards of your furniture before it agrees to take your property on to its books.

TELEVISION LICENCES
Do you need a special licence?
- **Yes** – if you offer self-catering accommodation and have installed television sets in your properties, you should apply for a Hotel and Mobile Units Television Licence ('hotel licence').

Despite its name, the hotel licence encompasses accommodation ranging from hotels, guesthouses, bed and breakfasts and inns to holiday cottages, flats and chalets, and even to camping and caravan sites.

The TV Licensing Authority says that you should always take out a hotel licence if you are providing televisions for the use of guests. While staying on your property, guests are not covered by their home licence.

The fee for the licence is determined by the number of guest units in which you have installed or intend to install television sets. If this number is no more than 15, the fee is the same as a standard domestic licence fee.

THE TRADE DESCRIPTIONS ACT 1968

Does this apply to me?

Yes – if you are either:

(a) advertising your accommodation facilities in a brochure or any other form of advertising material (including the web), or

(b) making statements about your facilities to the public.

What does the Act cover?

This Act states that it is an offence for you to knowingly or recklessly make 'false statements' about any facilities or services offered by you.

What constitutes a false statement?

Examples of false statements relating to accommodation facilities could include statements made about the quality, amenities and location of the accommodation premises or services related to it. For example, it would be a false statement if you advertised that your accommodation was 'five minutes from the beach' when it actually turns out that it is a half-hour drive, or that 'the rooms are spacious with panoramic views', when this applies only to one room.

Equally, the display of a sign or logo to which you are not entitled could constitute a false statement. For example, if you were to display on your premises an incorrect VisitBritain Star rating, or an outdated tourist board rating such as a Key classification and grading, this could be regarded as a breach of the Act.

Misrepresentation

Making false statements can result not only in a criminal prosecution under the Trade Descriptions Act, it may also result in a civil claim being brought against you by any person who has suffered loss as a result of a false statement. This stems from what is referred to in law as misrepresentation.

Misrepresentation occurs where a party is induced to enter into a contract by certain statements that later turn out to be untrue. With respect to accommodation premises, such statements could again include ones about the quality, amenities and location of the property. For example, if Mr Anderson and his family had booked into your self-catering property with an assurance from you that it was only 'five minutes from the beach', and it turned out to be a half-hour drive, he would be able to either (i) refuse to continue with the booking and claim damages from you for any losses incurred as a result, or (ii) continue staying with you but claim damages for his and his family's distress and disappointment.

Price statements
Does this apply to me?
Almost certainly yes – as the relevant law (the Consumer Protection Act 1987) covers all statements of price whether in an advertisement, a brochure, a leaflet or on the web, or those given by letter or orally in person or over the telephone, it will normally apply to all accommodation providers.

What does the Act say?
This Act makes it a criminal offence for accommodation providers, amongst others, to give guests misleading information on the prices charged for accommodation and any related facilities, services or goods ('misleading price indications').

The Act also makes it an offence not to do everything reasonably possible to correct a price indication that has subsequently become misleading if it is reasonable to assume that customers will still be relying on the original price information.

THE DISABILITY DISCRIMINATION ACT
The Disability Discrimination Act (the DDA) was introduced in 1995 to help end the discrimination that many disabled people face in their day-to-day lives. To ensure this, the Act gives disabled people new rights of access to goods, facilities and services, which includes tourist accommodation. These rights are enforceable by any disabled individual through the courts, if necessary.

Legal considerations
- PLANNING PERMISSION AND BUILDING REGULATIONS
- BUSINESS RATES
- LETTING OPTIONS FOR SELF-CATERING ACCOMMODATION
- PRIVATE WATER SUPPLIES
- THE RESALE OF GAS AND ELECTRICITY
- HEALTH AND SAFETY
- INSTALLING AND MAINTAINING GAS APPLIANCES
- ELECTRICAL EQUIPMENT
- GENERAL PRODUCT SAFETY
- FIRE SAFETY OF FURNITURE IN SELF-CATERING ACCOMMODATION
- TELEVISION LICENCES
- THE TRADE DESCRIPTIONS ACT 1968
- THE DISABILITY DISCRIMINATION ACT

Does the Act apply to me?

Yes – if you provide any sort of accommodation, including self-catering.

How is 'disabled' defined?

Disabled people are all those whose physical and mental impairments have a substantial and long-term adverse effect on their ability to carry out normal, day-to-day activities.

This includes those who have progressive conditions such as cancer, HIV, multiple sclerosis and muscular dystrophy, and who are likely to become increasingly disabled by their illness over time. These people become covered by the Act when their condition causes a noticeable effect on their ability to undertake day-to-day activities.

How does the Act impact on me?

The two most relevant parts of the Act relate to employment and access to goods, facilities and services. Your responsibilities are set out below.

Employment

You are required to treat disabled employees or job applicants the same as any other applicants. This covers all areas of employment, including recruitment, terms and conditions, promotion and transfers, training and development and the dismissal process.

Access to goods, facilities and services

As a 'service provider', you need to make sure you treat disabled guests the same as you treat other guests, unless there is adequate justification for less favourable treatment, such as health and safety reasons. You would be treating disabled guests less favourably if you (i) refuse to serve them, (ii) offer less favourable terms, or (iii) offer a lower standard of service compared with what you normally offer. If you treat someone less favourably, the Act allows them to seek damages from you through the county court.

You are also required to make reasonable adjustments to the way you deliver your services to make it easier for disabled guests to use them. If, for example, it is impossible or unreasonably difficult for a disabled person to use one of your services, you may need to change the relevant underlying practice, policy, or procedure to make it easier, or provide an alternative method of making your services available (this provision does not require you to physically change your premises). Before you make any changes, it is advisable to check that your adjustments are appropriate with a disabled person or disability organisation.

You are only required to do what is 'reasonable'. Service providers do have flexibility when considering how to make their services accessible to disabled people. All circumstances would be considered when interpreting what is reasonable, including the cost, its practicality, and the extent of a service provider's resources. What might be considered reasonable for a large multi-unit self-catering holiday park operator may not be so for an individual cottage owner.

You will have a duty as a 'service provider' to take reasonable steps to remove, alter or avoid any physical barriers that make it impossible or unreasonably difficult for disabled people to make full use of your facilities, if the service cannot be provided by an alternative method.

If you are planning building work or refurbishment, you could include disability-related changes at the same time. You are advised to contact the planning or building department of your local authority for advice before carrying out any such work.

National Accessible Scheme

The National Accessible Scheme recognises and identifies those places to stay that meet the needs of people with disabilities. For further information please contact Quality in Tourism (details in Sources of further help).

Next chapter

Now that you are aware of the regulations and you have worked through the process of the suitability of your property, you can start to plan your venture. In your mind you may now have an idea of the target market you hope to attract and the standard that you want to achieve.

Legal considerations

- PLANNING PERMISSION AND BUILDING REGULATIONS
- BUSINESS RATES
- LETTING OPTIONS FOR SELF-CATERING ACCOMMODATION
- PRIVATE WATER SUPPLIES
- THE RESALE OF GAS AND ELECTRICITY
- HEALTH AND SAFETY
- INSTALLING AND MAINTAINING GAS APPLIANCES
- ELECTRICAL EQUIPMENT
- GENERAL PRODUCT SAFETY
- FIRE SAFETY OF FURNITURE IN SELF-CATERING ACCOMMODATION
- TELEVISION LICENCES
- THE TRADE DESCRIPTIONS ACT 1968
- THE DISABILITY DISCRIMINATION ACT

All this information should help you decide where you want to position yourself and in turn will guide you in not making costly mistakes whilst getting your property ready and equipped.

In the next chapter we detail how you should go about launching your property. We review considerations you should have with regard to preparing the property, advertising and getting graded.

Chapter 3
Equipping the unit

By now you will have obtained the necessary planning permission (if required) and are confident that you are aware of and will meet all the legal requirements so that you can go ahead with the exciting part of converting, adapting and equipping your self-catering property. However, before you get deep into organising builders, planning interior design features and purchasing bed linen and teapots, there is another priority issue to start working on.

The importance of quality

Although at this stage you may not have started on converting, decorating or equipping your self-catering property, you will need to think about some of the requirements that may affect how you will advertise and promote your business.

The importance of quality

- VISITBRITAIN'S NATIONAL QUALITY ASSURANCE SCHEME (NQAS)

VISITBRITAIN'S NATIONAL QUALITY ASSURANCE SCHEME (NQAS)

For any prospective visitor, looking through an accommodation guide to find a suitable property can be bewildering. VisitBritain and many local authorities produce annual accommodation guides, which are also linked to their websites. In order that you can advertise with these organisations, you need to have your property assessed under VisitBritain's National Quality Assurance Schemes (NQAS). These schemes cover all types of accommodation, not just self-catering, and provide assurance to guests that the advertised accommodation is meeting a recognised standard. The scheme awards ratings according to quality. The higher the quality of the accommodation is, the higher the rating.

It can be useful to decide on the quality rating you would like and then work towards it. The rating will depend on many factors, both tangible and intangible. This will include the quality of beds and bedding, the style and quality of furniture, and spaciousness of rooms. All of these points are assessed in more detail later. However, it is worth asking yourself whether you want to be a top-quality self-catering property or whether, realistically, your property lends itself more to attracting the middle market.

Now will be an important time to obtain a copy of the NQAS standards to ensure that, as you continue to plan your property and begin to equip it, you do so to maximise your rating under NQAS. The NQAS standards list the minimum requirements throughout your property, from bed sizes to furniture. This is the absolute minimum standard required. The NQAS does not require you to do anything extraordinary, but simply ensures that guests can use your accommodation safely and appropriately. However, to achieve a higher rating you may want to enhance overall quality standards by offering more than the minimum. To obtain a copy of the NQAS standards contact Quality in Tourism (details in Sources of further help).

Case study
An Inspector Calls

We are often referred to as 'inspectors', but a more accurate description of us is 'assessors'. The very idea of 'inspecting' something brings with it the notion of seeing if something is 'up to standard', and criticising it if it's not. That is not what we are about. I, along with a team of colleagues, will assess a property as it stands and operates, awarding a rating based on the quality of the property and its position in the marketplace.

You cannot tell if something is good unless you have seen a range of properties, and a major part of our training involves seeing all sorts of establishments. These range from those with a basic acceptable standard through to the truly excellent. These

---

standards are set by the industry and based on the customer's expectations. There would be no way that I could make an assessment unless I had seen what now runs to hundreds of different self-catering properties.

What happens on an assessment? I do not stay in the property, as that would be impractical, so an appointment is made with the owner, or their agent, to assess the property when it is most appropriate, usually when it is not occupied. Prior to my visit I will have requested the brochure and any information that is sent out to visitors. This can have quite an impact on the guest and forms the initial part of the assessment, which I will note along with the quality of all aspects of the accommodation. This does not only mean the intrinsic and physical quality, but the thought that has been put into considering the comfort and convenience of the guest. Again, the assessment is based on the comparison with the best practice in other like self-catering properties.

The owner or agent usually accompanies me as I look both outside and in. Although I am not staying in the unit, I will strip at least one of the beds as well as open drawers and wardrobes. Because a kitchen is often the most important room for the guest I will, amongst other things, be looking at the crockery, utensils and also the inside of the oven. I then debrief on every facet of the property, from the inventory through to any additional facilities such as a laundry or games room.

It's very rewarding to recognise and acknowledge some of the really good quality points, and there are always some. However, what may also come from the debrief are the identification of areas where quality could be enhanced and developed further, often at low cost and to the potential benefit of the guest and operator alike. It's important to note that quality recommendations are 'could-do' and not 'must-do'. The last thing I want to do is tell an operator how to run their business. We work in partnership and do not 'police' the industry.

The importance of quality

- VISITBRITAIN'S NATIONAL QUALITY ASSURANCE SCHEME (NQAS)

Any recommendations are based on examples from similar operators and not based on personal opinions. It's amazing how objective you become in this job. I didn't think that would be the case when I first became an assessor (as a poacher turned gamekeeper). However, one thing that I and a lot of self-catering operators have come to appreciate is that things are always changing and developing because quality, like guest's expectations, never stands still.

I put the points that we discuss into a written report for the operator. They receive this along with their certificate showing their rating after the visit. This rating helps tell the guest that your property has been independently assessed and has received an official endorsement from VisitBritain.

External features

Some of the initial points that you should consider when looking at your property's external features are parking, entrances and gardens. You also need to ensure that all external aspects of your property are well maintained.

PARKING AND DRIVEWAYS

Safe parking is a main consideration for many guests when deciding which property they want to stay in. Being able to park close to the property just to unload when they first arrive will be helpful, especially as some cottages, urban flats and apartments may not have a dedicated parking area.

If you have a number of units, it will be important that each has its own designated parking area. Take into account that friends and family will often holiday together and this may mean that there could be two cars per unit. Defining the space for each unit will help to prevent any potential problems. Creating safe parking may take away some of the garden, but it is an important matter to consider in the planning stage.

Where a garage is available this should be easily accessible and door opening uncomplicated. Visitors should also be able to access the property easily, and driveways or entrances should be clear. The drive should be without potholes, and paved areas need to be swept clean. Regular pressure washing will help to eliminate green slippery surfaces. For visitors arriving late or in low season, you need to ensure that they can find the property easily. Sensor lighting can be very effective, more so than depending on someone to leave an outside light on after preparing the unit.

External features

- PARKING AND DRIVEWAYS

- GARDENS

- MAINTAINING THE EXTERIOR

- NEIGHBOURS

GARDENS

Providing a garden for visitors to relax in will be an added bonus, but you need to consider that gardens can be high maintenance. The garden will often be the first impression any guest receives of the property, so it is important that lawns, flowerbeds, containers and baskets are all neat and well tended. You may need to employ a gardener or, if you intend to manage the property yourself, this will be an additional task for changeover day.

The style of the garden may depend on whether you plan to take children, who may want to play football, or if you will allow dogs. Any play equipment needs to be sturdy, safe and regularly maintained and furniture provided should be clean – no bird droppings or leftover debris from previous visitors. Garden furniture is available in a wide range of styles and quality – plastic may be easy to keep clean and replace but wood may look better, although it can be heavy to move and may need regular treatment to appear its best.

Planters and containers need less attention than larger gardens, but they will still need regular watering and a weekly drink may not be sufficient. If maintaining a garden is not possible, providing a patio area with seating could be an alternative. Think about the type of hard surface that you use, as some types of stone and decking can become slippery when wet.

As visitors will often use gardens late into the evening, sensor or switched lighting would be a useful consideration. Patio heaters can also make a difference to visitors during the cooler evenings, but these need to be safe and easy to operate. If you are able to provide a barbecue, it will need to be sturdy, clean and ready to use. You will need to consider the type of fuel (gas or charcoal) and whether this will be included in the rental, and include instructions for lighting. Some visitors will be pleased to use the barbecue for much of their holiday, whilst others may not touch it. Cleaning the barbecue could also be an additional heavy chore that is time-consuming on changeover day.

Storage of barbecues and garden furniture will also need to be considered. Many types of furniture can be left out all year, but if you intend to provide seat cushions these can take up a lot of space. You are also dependent upon visitors not leaving them out in the rain on the evening before and day of changeover! A spare set may be a necessity.

If your location is likely to attract walkers, cyclists or birdwatchers it will be helpful to have a shed or outbuilding as a storage area. Cyclists will need somewhere safe to keep their bikes, and an outbuilding is also useful for boots, wet clothing and play equipment, as well as the barbecue and garden furniture. But make sure your outbuilding is not used as storage for clutter! Remember also the washing line or whirligig. Check regularly for breaks and make sure that there is a sufficient supply of pegs.

MAINTAINING THE EXTERIOR

All external aspects of the property should be well maintained. Check gutters for a build-up of leaves, check for loose roof tiles and check that water butts are not covered in slime. Consider how first impressions are affected by oil or calor gas tanks and consider whether you could screen them.

NEIGHBOURS

Not many holiday properties are situated in isolated locations without neighbours and many could be linked or in close proximity to other residents.

It is therefore very important to take your neighbours into consideration in the planning stages of preparing your property. Using effective screening, hedging or fencing between shared gardens will help to create privacy for both parties. Noise and disturbance may be difficult to avoid in the garden, but fitting as much insulation as possible inside the property should help to absorb some of the sound.

Planning the interior

Now that you have given thought to the exterior, you can turn your attention to the interior of your property and the ways that you can design it to maximise your business.

PLANNING THE LAYOUT

To help you design the interior of your property, consider making scale drawings of all the rooms. Then position (again to scale) all the furnishings you plan to have for each room. If you are starting from scratch with a blank canvas, it will be easier to design each room's layout. It may be tempting to use some previously owned furniture and furnishings, but be careful if you do contemplate this. You may think you are saving money, and initially you might be, but a holiday is an expensive purchase and visitors may not be thrilled with a collection of mismatched and variable-quality standards of furniture and equipment. Your ultimate aim is to attract repeat business and referrals but this will not occur if you try to cut corners.

DECORATION

Decoration of your property will be about getting the balance right. However you decide to decorate, consider how easy it will be to maintain. Wallpaper can be patterned, embossed or textured but should be a suitable design to be damp wiped. Textured finished wallpaper will have the benefit of helping to disguise slightly irregular wall and ceiling surfaces. This can be especially useful in older properties. If you use wallpaper, bear in mind that there may be the occasional tear when luggage or furniture is moved. Keep some spare rolls to patch up damaged areas. It will be a lot easier than wallpapering every twelve months.

Painted walls should prove a lot easier to maintain, as you will only have to touch up scuffmarks as they happen, but remember to buy more paint than you initially require for this. It is relatively easy to add interest with special paint effects

External features

- PARKING AND DRIVEWAYS
- GARDENS
- MAINTAINING THE EXTERIOR
- NEIGHBOURS

Planning the interior

- PLANNING THE LAYOUT
- DECORATION
- FLOORING
- FURNITURE
- SOFT FURNISHINGS
- LIGHTING
- HEATING
- ACCESSORIES
- DINING AREA

and other relief. Colour can also be used to play tricks on the eye. Painting a high ceiling in a dark colour can make it appear lower and using a dark colour on opposite walls can help a wide room seem narrower. It can also be less expensive to change the appearance of a room should you want to refresh the decoration, or change colours to suit current fashions.

As well as decorating the rooms, consider additional relief that can help lift their appearance, add interest and enhance the character of the accommodation. Adding skirtings will protect the walls from damage by furniture and when the floor is vacuumed. A dado rail will also protect a wall from knocks from the back of a chair and provides a natural break in the wall's colour scheme. A picture rail can be effective in allowing pictures to be easily moved around without knocking more holes in the wall. They also provide a visual break in rooms with high ceilings.

Pictures can provide the finishing touch and can help add character and interest. For example, in a rural self-catering property, the pictures may all be of local scenes. Mirrors are also useful as they can not only make a small room feel larger, but also provide a useful accessory for guests wherever they are located.

FLOORING

Floor coverings will be among the more expensive purchases you may make so you need to consider what you provide carefully. Your ultimate choice may be affected by the style of your property as well as your market and tariff.

Floor coverings have to withstand a good deal of wear and tear, so choosing what to use is important. Fashion trends have helped to make laminate and stripped wood flooring more popular and both these styles are easy to maintain. Carpeting will help to insulate and absorb noise and comes in a wide range of quality and prices. Just in the same way that a bed base enhances the comfort of the bed mattress, so the quality of underlay will make a large difference to the overall quality of the carpet. Whatever style of flooring you decide on, it should always be professionally fitted. That does not necessarily mean you need to pay to have someone fit it for you, but it does mean that carpet should be stretched and fitted correctly to the edges of the floor and laminate should not have any gaps between sections.

Certain areas of your property will take quite a lot of wear and tear, so floor covering in such areas as an entrance hall will need to be hard wearing. Consider fitting a high-quality doormat to reduce wear at entrances and by French windows.

FURNITURE

You will need sufficient easy seating to accommodate the maximum number of occupants. Armchairs and sofas need be comfortable but they will also take a lot of wear and tear – latex filling can be more resilient than feather. Consider the style of furniture. If you are appealing to an older market, then low, very soft sofas may prove impractical. If you are appealing to a more discerning market, then old-fashioned wing backed armchairs may be inappropriate. You may also consider having loose covers that can be easily cleaned.

Occasional tables and bookshelves may add character and provide useful storage space. Consider adding coasters if you have any vulnerable surfaces, although a resilient polyurethane-based finish may prove to be more practical.

SOFT FURNISHINGS

Window coverings, whether they are curtains or blinds, should be easy to draw. Corded pulls can present some problems to visitors and replacements could be expensive. Interlining the curtains will help create more effective 'blackout' and will insulate and enhance their appearance. Swags and tiebacks can also add to the visual effect, but take into account extra work and cleaning on changeover day.

LIGHTING

Effective lighting is essential if guests are going to be able to use your property with ease. Lighting needs not only to provide overall general illumination, but also needs to meet the various needs of the visitor. Consider the location of wall or ceiling lights. Consider where switches will be to ensure they can be turned on and off easily. You may want double switches, so a light can be turned on from two different rooms or positions.

Table lamps and standard lamps can be positioned around a room to create suitable light levels, allowing TV to be watched by some family members whilst others read. Dimmer switches can be very effective in the sitting and dining rooms, and shades can be helpful in diffusing the light, but be careful: lampshades are like magnets for dust, especially those with fringe tassels. Consider also using low-energy light bulbs. These can save you money in the longer term.

HEATING

Heating comes in many different designs, from warm-air circulation using floor level ducts, to electric radiators, storage radiators and, more commonly, central heating. Whatever form of heating you have, consider how easy it is to use. Easily controlled heating will allow guests to be comfortable throughout their stay. If you have a thermostatic valve on each radiator the guest will be able to set the room temperature exactly as they want it. If you have an open fire, be sure to provide fire irons and sufficient fuel or kindling. Where there is a wood burner, remember to provide operating instructions; it may be the first time a guest has used one. Many self-catering properties do not have central heating. If you have storage heaters or, as often found in bathrooms, a fan heater, consider whether it is easy to operate.

Air conditioning is not generally found in self-catering properties and would not be expected by the guest, but providing a fan for those warm summer days would be a very helpful addition and would be a bonus during hot spells.

ACCESSORIES

Any electrical accessories you provide will need to be conveniently positioned close to a plug point, but also easy to reach and use. A radio on a high shelf or a television trapped between two armchairs may not be convenient to either reach or watch. Consider also that guests may need plug points to recharge mobile telephones, use a hairdryer or connect a camcorder. Having sufficient plug points will be important to ensure guests' needs are met.

As well as ensuring that the television is in a position that your guests can easily view it, you may need to consider providing satellite or cable TV where a signal is not available, or is inconsistent. Whichever is provided, there should be details on the available channels. Also, keep a close eye on remote controls – they will need to be checked regularly for batteries, which can have a habit of going missing.

DINING AREA

In the dining area (which may be a separate room or part of the sitting room or kitchen) you will need a sufficiently large enough table and adequate chairs for all the occupants to sit down together. Remember that the table needs to be sturdy and able to withstand wet wiping and hot coffee cups – a polyurethane coating could help to prevent some marking. Seat pads on wooden seats will add to comfort, but be aware that the pads can sometimes become detached from the tiebacks and they will need regular washing.

Kitchen

The kitchen can be the most important room for visitors taking a self-catering holiday. Although many guests will eat out most nights, for some, especially those with children, it provides a welcome opportunity to prepare and cook fresh meals. It is therefore important to take into consideration the overall design, practicality and range of equipment in the kitchen.

SPACE

The amount of available space will often dictate what can be provided. Not every kitchen can accommodate a dishwasher or a separate freezer. It will also be helpful to take into account the number of occupants to ensure there is ample storage space for guests' food. Be careful not to overfill cupboards with kitchen equipment and don't clutter work surfaces.

Planning the interior

- PLANNING THE LAYOUT
- DECORATION
- FLOORING
- FURNITURE
- SOFT FURNISHINGS
- LIGHTING
- HEATING
- ACCESSORIES
- DINING AREA

Kitchen

- SPACE
- FLOORING
- UNITS
- WHITE GOODS
- OTHER EQUIPMENT
- CROCKERY, CUTLERY AND UTENSILS

FLOORING

Kitchen flooring needs to be durable and able to withstand knocks, scuffs and spills. Importantly it also needs to be non-slip and washable. Flooring quality ranges from stone or ceramic tiles, to wood, laminate and vinyl flooring. Tiling may be the highest quality, but breakages can easily occur when items are dropped. Vinyl may be less expensive and, if cushioned, can be comfortable underfoot, but can also split, mark and dent easily.

UNITS

Kitchen units and work surfaces also come in a wide range of styles and quality. Again, take into account that they need to be sturdy and robust. A flimsy hinge will soon cause doors to drop. Where space is limited and unit cupboards have to be fitted into corners, consider incorporating swivel or pull-out shelves to create more storage.

Work surfaces will need to be robust enough to cope with knife marks and perhaps a hot saucepan. Granite and wood will be more expensive, and will they cope with this type of accident? More economical worktops can be more suitable, but consider the colour – a plain, pale colour may show up marks more easily than a mottled dark colour.

WHITE GOODS

The choice of cookers and ovens is extensive, from simple freestanding ovens to an expensive AGA. You need to consider both the overall quality of the oven and how easy it will be for the visitor to use. An AGA, although it may be of high quality and look wonderful, may not be easy for a novice user. The oven needs to be of large enough capacity to accommodate enough roasting dishes for the number of visitors. The more guests you accommodate, the more oven space they will need. Indeed, you may even need to consider providing two ovens. Consider also self-cleaning ovens. On changeover day these can save you a lot of time.

Microwaves can be very simple or very complicated and range in price accordingly. Consider how easy they are to use and, as with all equipment, ensure that operating instructions are readily available. With some lets, you may find that this has been the only oven used.

The amount of available space will usually affect what you can provide, so if you are not able, or decide it is unnecessary to provide a separate freezer, you will need to provide a fridge with an ice-making compartment. Many guests will bring or buy frozen food, so consider the capacity before purchasing your fridge/freezer. Most larder fridges and many freezers defrost automatically, which will help with cleaning.

Other white goods that you need to consider will also depend on the type of guest staying and available space. Some guests will want a dishwasher, especially if they have one at home. Indeed, for a large self-catering unit, it can be essential. It can also be very useful on changeover day, if you discover a pile of dirty dishes.

A washing machine and tumble dryer will be especially useful for families with young children and babies, as well as for guests on an outdoor holiday, such as walkers, cyclists and fishermen. If space is at a premium, consider getting a combined washer/dryer.

Efficient extraction is vital in a kitchen, especially if it is small. Even a small cooker hood can make a difference, although you will need to ensure that it is cleaned regularly. Extraction can have added importance in combined lounge/diners.

OTHER EQUIPMENT

Other basic requirements include a toaster and kettle, amongst other items. There is a vast choice in designs and prices, but as with other items in the kitchen, ensure they have sufficient capacity and can be easily cleaned on changeover day.

CROCKERY, CUTLERY AND UTENSILS

A wide range of crockery, cutlery and utensils are provided in self-catering properties and the NQAS standards booklet details the minimum requirement necessary. However, as with quality elsewhere in the holiday home, meeting the minimum requirement will not necessarily provide a high quality grade. For example, matching crockery is a

Kitchen

- SPACE
- FLOORING
- UNITS
- WHITE GOODS
- OTHER EQUIPMENT
- CROCKERY, CUTLERY AND UTENSILS

requirement of the scheme, but whether you purchase inexpensive dishes or bone china cups and saucers will depend on the market you are trying to meet and the level of quality you are aiming to achieve.

Additional crockery and cutlery can also be very useful. If you have a property for two guests, provide at least four of everything so they do not have to wash up all of the time, or operate the dishwasher with a half load. Consider providing additional items that guests may find useful, such as extra chopping boards (for meat and fish), a garlic press and a knife sharpener. A list of extras could be very long, but think what you have in your own home and what is useful. A jar lid-opener, peppermill and hot pan stand are just a few ideas.

The NQAS standards also require you to provide a fire extinguisher or a fire blanket as well as smoke detectors. With the latter, consider where they are placed, as the cooker or toaster can easily set them off. With the former, extinguishers will need to be inspected regularly as the pressure can drop.

Bedrooms

When deciding on how to furnish your bedrooms you will need to consider not only how many guests you want to accommodate, but also the quality you wish to convey and the ease of use of your guests.

PLANNING THE BEDROOM

The shape of the bedroom will have a big impact on how the room will be designed, where the bed will be positioned and where other furniture will be placed. Some basic considerations should include being able to get in and out of bed with ease. If you have squeezed a double bed into a room which is really only suitable for a single bed, can both guests get in and out of bed without having to climb over one another? Placing double beds up against walls may be acceptable for your own use, but it may be inconvenient for guests in your self-catering property. With twin beds you might consider placing them against the wall with a gap in between, but you may want to avoid placing them side by side. This will place guests who want to sleep in separate beds very close together, which is not always acceptable.

Bear in mind the height of ceilings and also sloping ceilings, which are evident in loft conversions. Alcoves may not be able to take freestanding furniture, but built-in units could be a suitable way of utilising the space. Consider how much free space will be available after you have furnished and equipped the room. Remember that guests will need storage space not only for clothing, but also for their cases and bags. If a room is crammed full and there is no suitable area for luggage, other furniture may have to be used, such as the top of wardrobes.

You also need to consider the ease of use for the guest. Can the guest open and close all drawers and wardrobe doors? If the wardrobe has been placed so close to the bed it cannot be easily opened it creates frustration. Similarly, guests may want to open windows and access should not be blocked by furniture.

BEDS

The requirements of a self-catering property catering for a succession of different guests are very different from buying a bed for personal use in a domestic situation. Beds should be of suitable quality to ensure greater durability and guest comfort.

The composition of a bed is quite complex and there is a huge choice available. A spring interior mattress could be open coil, continuous springs or pocket; a non-sprung mattress could be latex, foam or fibre. The base is equally vital and could be boarded, firm-edge base, sprung-edge base, slatted base, metal base or storage base. It is important to remember that a mattress and a base work together to achieve support and comfort. When buying a bed, you should always consider the two together and ensure that the mattress and base complement each other.

Supplementary beds are often used in self-catering properties. These can be wall beds, sofa beds and folding beds. Often these are really only suitable for children as they usually only have thin foam mattresses. All of these beds need to be checked regularly and visitors provided with instructions on how to open them. These styles of beds may also require non-standard size bedding.

The National Bed Federation and the website www.sleepcouncil.com (01756 791089) are able to offer help and guidance in the choice and care of beds.

WHICH SIZE OF BED SHOULD YOU HAVE?

When designing your self-catering property you will need to take into account the number of guests you will accommodate to obtain the best flexibility. Try to achieve the best combination of beds and types of bedrooms.

This will, of course, depend on the size of the rooms. If space allows for two single beds, then this twin-room arrangement can be a very flexible option. It can accommodate a single guest, two guests travelling together, or possibly a couple. Another consideration would be to have zip and link beds. Although initially they can be more expensive to purchase, zip and link beds can offer the best option. They allow a twin room to be made into a very comfortable double room, creating a king-sized double bed when two 3' single beds are zipped together. However, if you choose zip and link beds, be careful in your choice, as the singles can be either 2'6" or 3'. It is doubtful that a 2'6" bed will meet the expectations of two large adult guests if the room is sold as a twin. This may not cause a complaint, but it will almost certainly cause disappointment.

Twin rooms usually need a little extra space compared to double-bedded rooms, to allow for manoeuvring beside and between the beds. If the bedroom is slightly smaller, consider whether it can accommodate a standard double bed (4'6" wide), a king-sized bed (5') or a super king-sized bed (6'). Be aware that bed sizes and names are widely used but not standard and always check dimensions/names with the supplier. Alternatively, bunk beds are great fun for children, but you will need to ensure that they are safe and that the top bunk is not near to light fittings or windows.

SHOULD THE BED HAVE A HEADBOARD?

Not all beds come with a fitted headboard and you will need to have one, not only for the guest's comfort, but also to protect your walls. Headboards prevent the bed from moving away from the wall if the guest sits up in bed and will stop the pillow from falling down the back of the bed. Consider what type of headboard will be most suitable. A wooden or brass frame headboard may suit the bed frame, but a padded board may be more comfortable. Consider also that if you purchase a fabric-covered headboard it may get marked and need more maintenance.

WHAT TYPE OF BEDDING AND PILLOWS SHOULD YOU USE?

Mattress and pillows will need to be covered by washable protectors, and if you use a quilted design this can enhance a guest's comfort further. You may be considering waterproof protectors on children's beds. Do not be tempted to place them on adult beds. These prevent the body from 'breathing' properly and usually make the guest sweat, especially in hotter weather, making for a very uncomfortable night's sleep. If you feel you must use a plastic mattress protector, consider placing additional padding between it and the bottom sheet to enhance comfort.

Some guests may be allergic to down duvets and feather pillows, so it may be worthwhile also having synthetic, non-allergenic duvets and pillows available. Guests will usually tell you in advance when they have this nature of special request.

DUVETS OR BLANKETS?

You can find both duvets and blankets being used in self-catering properties. Duvets tend to be more popular, but it is important to remember tog ratings – it may not be conducive to sleep under a 13-tog rating in the middle of summer. The split tog ratings are excellent, but you will need extra space to store them. If you plan to use linen and blankets, there are other considerations. Linen could be made of natural fibres, man-made or a mix. Egyptian cotton with a high thread count is perhaps the best quality, but will it be suitable and appropriate when you take into account the laundering and ironing? Polyester/cotton may be prone to pilling but is less expensive and easier to wash and dry.

With regard to colours you might want to use practical all-white linen throughout, as it is interchangeable, or a coordinated colour for each room to tie in with the decoration.

If you opt for blankets, these come in a variety of types and quality, ranging from cellular weave, cotton waffle and acrylic fleece, through to all wool, lambswool and cashmere. Whatever you choose, it will require regular dry cleaning. If you provide spare blankets, consider storing these in the wardrobe for guest use if needed. If placed in a zipped bag the presentation of these will be higher than if just left loose at the bottom of the wardrobe.

BEDROOM FURNITURE

The minimum bedroom furniture should include a wardrobe (or hanging area), drawers, bedside tables (or fixed shelves by the bed) and a dressing table with a mirror.

The requirement for a hanging space means that if space is very limited you do not have to provide a full, freestanding wardrobe. There should be enough hanging space for four coat hangers per person, and this can be achieved by having a hanging rail across the corner of a room. It may not be an ideal situation, but would suffice. Adding a curtain would help screen the hanging rail and enhance appearances. Hanging rails that fix to the back of doors are also possible, although these need to allow free hanging. Simply hanging four items onto a hook is not suitable, as the clothes will get creased.

Consider also the range, usefulness and design of coat hangers. Wire hangers should be removed, as they do not allow clothes to hang well. Shaped wooden hangers often offer the best design, and non-slip trouser hangers and padded hangers for blouses offer additional choice and convenience. Matching sets of plastic hangers with skirt hooks provide a low-cost alternative.

If the bedside tables contain drawers then these can sometimes avoid the need for additional chests of drawers, also saving on space. If space is very limited beside the bed, consider fitting shelves instead of bedside tables.

The smallest shelf would need to be about the area of an A4 piece of paper, suitable for a pair of glasses, a glass of water and possibly a book.

You may have a dressing table with drawers and this can also avoid the need for having a separate chest of drawers. If you do place a dressing table in the bedroom, consider how easy it is to use. Can the guest sit at the 'table' comfortably and is there a kneehole? A dressing table with a kneehole is much more comfortable to sit at than one without. A dressing table with a mirror becomes easier to use and one with a table lamp is even further enhanced.

Always consider the intrinsic quality of the furniture you place into the property. A self-assembly wardrobe will not have the same durability or intrinsic quality as a solid one with good joinery. Think about the quality of chests of drawers or dressing tables and consider adding drawer liners to enhance both appearances and use. A mirror can be a small table mirror, but if you also provide a full-length mirror, or a large wall-mounted mirror, it enhances the guest's ease of use (and it can make the room appear larger).

BEDROOM FLOORING AND FURNISHINGS

The bedroom floor covering may not need to be as durable as in other parts of the unit, such as the entrance hall, and carpeting may be more appropriate than anything else, but think about colours and ease of cleaning. A small pattern or speckled background can certainly help to disguise minor marks.

Window dressing in bedrooms needs to be effective in excluding daylight and affording privacy. For example, if a bedroom faces east, will the early morning sun in mid-summer wake the guest up at a very early hour? This is a relatively small point, but could make the difference between a good night's sleep and a restless one. Consider also if you are going to use tiebacks for the curtains. If you do, they can enhance the appearance and hold the curtains away from the window, allowing more natural light into the room. Pelmets are another option.

Blinds are a popular alternative to curtains or can be used in conjunction with them. These can be especially useful to the guest in shielding the high-summer late afternoon sun, especially in a southwest-facing room. Bear in mind that guests may not always find it easy using blinds or curtains that are drawn by pull cords, so simpler designs can be more effective.

LIGHTING

Lighting in bedrooms needs to be intimate yet practical. It should be easy to control and appropriately sited. There should be lights by each bedspace, allowing guests to turn a light off easily when they go to bed and allowing them to turn a light on easily should they need to get up during the night. With double beds this means a light on each side of the bed, but with twin beds, the bedside light could be placed in between the beds, allowing each guest to reach it. Ideally though, if you can place the lights on the far side of each bed, then guests can switch their own light on without disturbing each other.

Guests may also want to read in bed and you should consider the location of bedside lights. If you have a bedside lamp that is lower than the guest's head when sitting in bed, the light bulb will blind them every time they switch the light on or off. If practical, try to have bedside lights that are positioned a little above head height when sitting in bed. You may decide that wall-mounted lights are best for this, or you may have tall lamps that meet this need.

Consider also the light controls. If you have wall lights, check that the light switches are in the right location to be easily reached from the bed. You may even dual-switch the main light with a switch by the bed for ease of use.

Lighting will also be useful by dressing tables, by mirrors and by the wardrobe. Consider when using each of these whether the guests stand in their own shadow or can see clearly. The overall amount of lighting you need will depend on the size and shape of your room, but try to ensure all areas are illuminated and provide a choice of lighting levels. Guests can always switch a light off if they want a more subdued ambience. Fitting dimmer switches may be the best option, giving guests full control over light levels.

Bathroom

Although guests will not spend as much time in the bathroom as they do in the bedroom, the bathroom remains a crucial part of the guest stay. The quality of the bathroom, the power of the shower, the amount of space to manoeuvre in and storage space, can all be memorable parts of their stay. Many guests will often clearly remember the quality of the bed and the quality of the shower or bath, often comparing (favourably) to that provided at home.

In this next section we look at the different aspects of the bathroom that make a guest stay comfortable.

DECORATION, FLOORING AND STORAGE

A fully tiled bathroom will usually be easier to maintain than one with painted or wallpapered walls. Mirrors will be important and a large mirror can be helpful as can a small shaving mirror. Consider where you place mirrors. If the washbasin is on one side of the room and the mirror is on the other, then someone having a wet shave will be to-ing and fro-ing between the two. If practical, you could even consider installing a heated mirror, which avoids misting.

Pictures and decorative objects can help lift the appearance of the bathroom, but be aware of damp conditions and provide those that are suited accordingly.

The right flooring is a less straightforward consideration. Carpeting can be very comfortable and warm underfoot and can be suitable in a domestic bathroom, but you need to consider that carpeting can become unhygienic with use and less easy to keep clean. With excessive damp it can quickly deteriorate. Flooring tiles may be more expensive and are often perceived as being higher quality, but can be very cold underfoot. Guests usually use the bathroom in bare feet, so comfort will be important. Some self-catering properties install underfloor heating beneath a tiled floor, and this can offer the best of both worlds. Vinyl flooring can be another alternative, being easy to maintain and less expensive.

Providing space for your guests' belongings is very often a neglected aspect. Will they have somewhere to place all their things? There may be a small shelf for their toothpaste and toothbrush, but what about all their other toiletries? Providing sufficient shelf space, hooks for cloths and rails for towels are all considerations to ensure the bathroom is easy to use for all your guests.

HEATING, AIR EXTRACTION AND LIGHTING

As in all other areas of the property, heating in bathrooms may vary. You may have central heating in the bathroom or an electric fan heater. Consider having a heated towel rail. This can be a real bonus during times when the central heating is not switched on and helps create a warm comfortable temperature and warm towels.

In all bathrooms, where there may be continual usage of the room over a period of time, an extractor fan will prove invaluable. Extractor fans help clear the mist after a shower or bath, reduce dust accumulation, helping to keep the room clean, and help prevent damp and all its associated problems, such as mildew and mould.

Enclosed lighting is a requirement for safety reasons. There should never be a bare light bulb in a bathroom. Effective illumination will be important, so consider where your lights are positioned. Clear lighting will be needed above the washbasin, for shaving. Recessed downlighters can be good because they are glare-free. Waterproof recessed light fittings above a shower cubicle can also be helpful.

It is worth mentioning that many guests who wear glasses obviously remove their glasses when in the bathroom. As a consequence, their vision is impaired and higher lighting levels rather than subdued lighting can be welcomed. A choice of light levels could be considered.

BATH OR SHOWER?

Space might dictate the range of fixtures you install in your bathroom. Can you install a shower and a bath, or just a shower? There are always some people who prefer one to the other. Showers do not usually use as much water as baths and are usually easier for someone with a disability, but baths can be more relaxing and are usually more suitable for children. For whatever you have or decide to install, it will be important to ensure that there is sufficient water pressure and ample hot water at the times when guests need it.

If you have space for a bath, then you can usually install a shower above. This should use up no more space, but you need to consider if the ceiling allows someone to stand comfortably under the showerhead. If your bathroom has a sloping ceiling, it may not work so effectively. A shower with an adjustable rail can be very useful, especially if a guest wants to avoid getting their hair wet.

If you do have a shower, ensure that it is one that is easy to use and does not cause sudden changes in water temperature. For baths that have a fixed shower attachment, it is worth considering a shower screen as opposed to a curtain. Although curtains are easily replaced, a screen is usually more efficient in helping to keep the floor dry. A shower curtain can also tend to wrap around the user, making them less user-friendly. Grab handles in baths and in shower cubicles will also be helpful to guests, especially if they have any difficulties moving.

Where possible, you could consider creating a wet room. This is very common in Europe and allows the guest to walk into a shower area of the bathroom where the floor slopes into a corner drain, avoiding the rest of the room from becoming wet. This can be especially helpful in creating a more accessible bathroom.

TOWELS AND TOILETRIES

If you decide to provide towels for your guests, and this can be included in the tariff or at an additional charge, then consider the quality of the towels provided. As with bed linen, the quality can vary. Absorbency, weight, texture and

Bathroom

- DECORATION, FLOORING AND STORAGE

- HEATING, AIR EXTRACTION AND LIGHTING

- BATH OR SHOWER?

- TOWELS AND TOILETRIES

- PLUMBING

softness are important aspects to consider. Also, how towelling wears after numerous washes will be important. Does it dry evenly or does it suffer from differential shrinkage because of patterned headers?

Consider also the range of towelling you provide. You may just provide a hand towel and a bath towel for each person, which would be sufficient. Or, depending on the type of guest you have staying and the type you want to attract, you might also want to provide a bath sheet, face cloth and a bathrobe. Consider also the colour of the towels. White towels can be popular, but if you have white towels in a mainly white bathroom with a white bathroom suite and white tiles, will someone with poor sight see them? It is worth considering using colour, allowing guests with poor sight to see things more clearly.

Guests are likely to bring a range of personal toiletries with them. However, as a minimum you should provide fresh soap for each guest. This does not have to be a fresh bar of soap, indeed that could get quite expensive, but could simply be liquid soap. You can get some very high-quality liquid soaps and, importantly for the guest, each time they push the dispenser they get fresh soap. Importantly for you, it creates less mess on the basin than a bar of soap and you just need to keep the bottle topped up to make it look fresh and new for each guest.

You could also consider providing additional toiletries, such as bath foam or salts, cotton wool, cotton buds and tissues. Remember to provide plenty of toilet paper, and consider the quality of it.

PLUMBING

For properties that are not connected to the mains sewerage system, or with small bore waste pipes, you will need to make guests aware of the plumbing. A card placed on the WC cistern or permanently fixed to the wall in a prominent place will hopefully help to prevent the later expense of a plumber.

Testing your property

Once you have finished decorating and furnishing your property you should question whether everything works as well as you planned. The best way to do this is to spend time in the property using all the equipment. Spend a night in each bedroom and use the bathroom yourself, not just once, but on an annual basis. Testing your rooms may seem unnecessary. Obviously you are familiar with them. After all, you designed them, decorated them and equipped them. But only by doing this will you be able to assess how easy everything is to use and where you might need to make changes.

TESTING THE BEDROOM

By sleeping in your own rooms you will see whether it is comfortable and convenient to use.

Start with the bed – is there sufficient space by the side of the bed, is the shared table between twin beds so small that there is only room for one teacup and is the bedside light at the right height? Are there adequate drawers to contain a reasonable amount of clothing? Can you open that wardrobe door or see yourself in the dressing table mirror? Is the carpet starting to wear in parts because it lacks underlay? When the curtains are drawn across the windows do they meet, or do they leave a gap? And, do they afford effective blackout? Can the temperature of the heating be independently controlled, and if so, is the thermostat accessible? If the guest wants to use the hairdryer, is there a mirror by a power point and does the full-length mirror need to be re-positioned? Is the television visible from only one chair?

TESTING THE BATHROOM

The same assessment could be carried out in the bathroom. Are the controls for the shower easy to operate and does the pressure alternate and affect the temperature? Is there a soap dish or suitable container on a shower wall? With a bath that also has an integral shower, does the spray from the head stay within the bath or will the floor be flooded? Is there good light intensity by a mirror for shaving or applying make-up and are there suitable surfaces for wash-bags and hooks for

Bathroom

- DECORATION, FLOORING AND STORAGE

- HEATING, AIR EXTRACTION AND LIGHTING

- BATH OR SHOWER?

- TOWELS AND TOILETRIES

- PLUMBING

Testing your property

- TESTING THE BEDROOM

- TESTING THE BATHROOM

- TESTING OTHER ROOMS

clothing? Is the extractor fan powerful enough to alleviate condensation and is there any supplementary heating such as a towel rail?

TESTING OTHER ROOMS

Similarly, assess the living and dining rooms and the kitchen. Can all areas be used with ease, is the microwave easy to operate, can the radio pick up all regular channels and is there a range of lighting levels in the living room?

Carrying out this self-assessment can be an eye-opener. A room-by-room 'ease of use' checklist will highlight what might not be working well and where there are points that could be developed. You will also be able to assess if the guests are likely to experience any intrusive noise, such as the central heating boiler. Ideally have the other rooms used by friends or family so that you can hear if noise from adjoining rooms is audible.

Replacement arrangements

In an ideal world nothing would break, fail to operate or be lost. But life is not like that and you need to prepare for eventualities.

SPARE SUPPLIES

Keep a spare set of easily changed items, for example, light bulbs, fuses and batteries for remote-control units or torches.

You should also consider having a supply of cutlery, crockery and utensils to replace any that get damaged or lost. You could keep these in a locked cupboard along with spare linen, pillows and cleaning materials, but when choosing crockery do not be tempted into buying a limited design range. Consider instead purchasing a duplicate set or choose a style that can be easily replaced and is widely available. The sales are often a good time to stock up on quality products such as linen and crockery.

REPAIRS

Keeping domestic appliances regularly serviced should also help to ensure that any slight problems are detected. It may be a sensible precaution to take out an extended service warranty on the more expensive white goods and electrical items.

For any unexpected problems, such as a faulty microwave, you are not likely to have a spare one to hand, but you will need to have made some plans to deal with the situation. If you do not manage the property yourself, you will need to ensure that your caretaker or cleaner is able to act on your behalf. Whatever situation you have, visitors will normally try to contact the owner if something goes wrong, and your contact details, or the details of your agent or cleaner needs to be clearly displayed in the unit.

HOW TO DEAL WITH DAMAGES

If you expect visitors to pay for damaged or lost items, you will need to make them aware on the terms and conditions of rental. Requesting them to leave some money for a replacement is probably a better idea than asking them to replace the item, otherwise you are likely to end up with a varied range of mismatched equipment.

Next chapter

The next chapter looks at how you can maximise bookings, from handling telephone enquiries to deciding on a policy for deposits. It takes you through the booking process and presents some considerations you may need to make when deciding on your operating policy.

Testing your property

- TESTING THE BEDROOM
- TESTING THE BATHROOM
- TESTING OTHER ROOMS

Replacement arrangements

- SPARE SUPPLIES
- REPAIRS
- HOW TO DEAL WITH DAMAGES

Chapter 4
Your operating policy

Running a self-catering property means that you are operating a business, and this requires you to set up systems to deal with enquiries, bookings and deposits. You will need to keep very detailed records and be sure that you are meeting all legal requirements. Before you consider creating an enquiry form, you need to think carefully through the terms and conditions that will form the contract between yourself and the hirer.

Setting terms and conditions

In setting terms and conditions you are making it clear to the visitors what they will receive in return for payment, what extras will have to be paid for, payment terms and cancellation terms. Unlike a B&B proprietor, you are providing a lot more than a bed, washing facilities and breakfast, so you need to have clear, concise terms and conditions. You need to ensure that there are no grey areas that could be open to a difference of opinion.

WHAT TO INCLUDE

This is a suggested list of things you may need to include in your terms and conditions:

- Payment, including the required deposit and how soon that has to be paid to secure the booking, and when the balance is due.
- What is included in the rate, such as fuel, electricity, linen, towels, etc.
- If there are any additional charges for facilities and their costs.

- The cancellation policy.
- The maximum number of occupants that can be accommodated.
- Whether you permit the occasional visitor and are prepared to provide a fold-up bed/bedding.
- Any policies regarding age of children, smoking, pets, single-gender groups.
- If pets are permitted, whether there are any restrictions on where they can go, and any financial liability for visitors for damage or mess.
- You will need to include the earliest arrival and latest departure times.
- Guests' responsibility for possessions and for leaving the property in a clean condition on departure.
- If you charge a housekeeping retainer, how much this is and how soon after their departure it will be returned.
- Your breakages or damages policy.
- Your own cancellation terms, e.g. if you were unable to provide the property because of a plumbing disaster or similar, would you offer a full refund or try to find a suitable alternative?

Setting terms and conditions

- WHAT TO INCLUDE

Dealing with enquiries

Having prepared the terms and conditions, you can now look at how you will take enquiries. You, as the owner, need to first consider the following points:

- Who will be answering the phone? (it may not always be you.)
- Will that person know what information to give?
- Will they know what information to ask for?
- How will they answer?
- Will the phone be switched on to the answer machine, or diverted to a mobile when you are out?

Dealing with enquiries

- THE IMPORTANCE OF ENQUIRIES
- SETTING UP A CHECKLIST
- CONVERTING ENQUIRIES INTO BOOKINGS
- RESPONDING TO ENQUIRIES
- WHAT IF YOU ARE OUT?

THE IMPORTANCE OF ENQUIRIES

It may seem a little like stating the obvious to talk about how to answer a telephone. However, a guest's first impression of your self-catering property will, on many occasions, be when they telephone. This may be to find out about the accommodation and availability, or hopefully to make a booking. This is a crucial point in the guest's journey as it is when they decide whether to make a reservation, or perhaps decide to try somewhere else.

SETTING UP A CHECKLIST

After a time, handling enquiries will become automatic for you, but it may not be so easy if others answer the phone. For all enquiries it is well worth keeping a checklist by the telephone with all the relevant questions to ask, as well as information on the unit(s). It should also include key points to tell the caller, such as the type of accommodation and any policies you may have regarding smoking, children or minimum ages, and then, of course, your prices. If you have a website, you can also mention this to the caller for further information, especially if it contains photographs which you know help to sell your property.

CONVERTING ENQUIRIES INTO BOOKINGS

Some telephone calls may simply be enquiries to check on availability and prices. It is not unusual for someone to ring a number of self-catering properties to compare prices and find the 'best deal'. This does not necessarily mean they are trying to find the cheapest place to stay and you should always consider an enquiry as a potential booking.

To convert an enquiry into a sale always emphasise any plus points. Never exaggerate but advise the caller of any special features or added convenience, for example, if your property is in its own grounds, has a secure garden or is close to shops. Whatever the feature is, it may be worth mentioning it as an 'upsell'. Do not underestimate an everyday feature, which you may take for granted.

RESPONDING TO ENQUIRIES

For all enquiries consider how you record the caller's details. Consider having a diary, an enquiry book or a standard form kept by the telephone. This can be printed off on a computer and, in addition to recording their name, address, telephone or mobile number or e-mail address, you can record the number in the party, including adults, children, babies and pets, and any special requests. It can also be very useful to record how they found out about you.

If the caller has given any indication of potential dates that they are interested in, record this as well. Try if possible to send your brochure immediately, as callers may often contact a number of properties for their details. You could even include with the brochure some relevant local information, such as leaflets on local attractions, or a 'what's on' guide. This could help convince them to book your accommodation as it illustrates extra care and attention, but you may want to be careful that the leaflets do not take the postage costs above that of a first-class stamp! You may also receive enquiries by letter and e-mail. These should also receive immediate attention.

If you receive a telephone enquiry but are unable to accommodate their required dates, still offer to send a brochure. You never know, after receiving the brochure they may prefer the look of your property and decide to change dates. Do not forget to include your current availability and always include a personalised letter with a brochure (a pre-formatted letter can be easily saved on the computer for this purpose). If you have a website or are linked to a local association, remember to give the caller the web address for further details.

WHAT IF YOU ARE OUT?

Although you are running a business from home there will be times when you are not going to be available to answer the telephone.

For these occasions you may want to consider transferring incoming calls to a mobile telephone so that you can always take the call. It may not always be convenient to deal with their enquiry there and then if you are in the middle of the supermarket, at the bank or walking the dog, but you can keep a notepad on you at all times, take their details and call them back as soon as you are home. Some operators and owners keep a small booking diary on them, so they can instantly advise callers if they have availability or not.

If diverting calls is going to be problematic, consider having an answer machine. These are perfectly acceptable. Do ensure that you respond to enquiries as soon as possible. Record a message that asks the caller to leave their name and

Dealing with enquiries

- THE IMPORTANCE OF ENQUIRIES
- SETTING UP A CHECKLIST
- CONVERTING ENQUIRIES INTO BOOKINGS
- RESPONDING TO ENQUIRIES
- WHAT IF YOU ARE OUT?

number and assures them that you will get back to them as soon as you are able. And don't forget, use the property name rather than the number if at all possible so the caller knows they have the right accommodation.

Bookings

You should consider having a simple system for dealing with all bookings efficiently and effectively. If you have just one property, a fairly basic system can be adopted, such as a large format diary. Alternatively, particularly if you have more than one unit, you could use a booking chart. This can be divided into columns with the calendar weeks in the left-hand column and the names of each unit along the top.

RECORDING BOOKINGS

In response to a telephone enquiry you may agree to pencil in a booking, but you will need to follow this up with a letter confirming a release date and verbally advise the caller that you can only provisionally hold the booking for an agreed period of time (this could be for two weeks). This is when a booking chart is invaluable – a provisional enquiry can be pencilled in and perhaps different coloured inks used to denote when a booking is confirmed, when the deposit is paid and when the balance is due and also paid. The chart can also include a column for extras or special requirements against the party name and how they found out about you. This latter point is very helpful when assessing the value of any advertising you have done.

Once a booking is made you will have entered into a contract. You need to be sure that customers understand your policies to avoid any confusion. Having a simple system should help to avoid any over-bookings or missed bookings, and it can record any special requests, such as a late arrival.

INFORMATION TO ASK FOR WHEN TAKING A BOOKING

You do not want to sound too officious when taking a booking but it is important that you get the necessary information from the caller and that you advise them of your policies. What time can they arrive, or will they be expecting to arrive late? If you have made arrangements for the key to be collected on arrival, is this communicated? It would not make a good impression if your guests arrive whilst you are in the middle of shopping and no-one is available to let them in.

You need to know if they have any special requirements and whether they know how to find you. By pre-empting these questions, and ensuring that you provide all the relevant information at the time of booking, you can ensure that your guests won't have the inconvenience of having to call you back. Information regarding any special requirements, such as advising if they have a mobility problem, will usually be volunteered, but the need for a 'special requirements' question can be very useful and will become apparent over time.

RESPONDING TO BOOKINGS

In response to receiving a deposit for a booking you will need to send an acknowledgement and receipt (for tax and accounting purposes). This will also give you the opportunity to confirm the dates of the booking, list any extras that have been requested or that they are required to bring and detail when the balance is due. Where bookings are made by e-mail, as is increasingly the case, this allows for an immediate response, although it is still a good idea to send an acknowledgement and receipt by post once a deposit is received. A reminder for the visitors to take out holiday insurance could also be included. This is often something that tourists do automatically when going abroad but does not seem to be considered so essential for holidays in the UK.

The final payment should also be acknowledged with a receipt and it is at this stage you can forward full directions to your property and any important information regarding access. Find out where the guests are coming from and how easy it will be for them to find you. Your brochure may already include a map identifying your general location, but you could send a route map from their location to yours to help them further. These are easily found on the Internet. Alternatively, you may want to send a more detailed location map showing your exact position, with clear directions. With written directions, use visual aids

Dealing with enquiries

- THE IMPORTANCE OF ENQUIRIES
- SETTING UP A CHECKLIST
- CONVERTING ENQUIRIES INTO BOOKINGS
- RESPONDING TO ENQUIRIES
- WHAT IF YOU ARE OUT?

Bookings

- RECORDING BOOKINGS
- INFORMATION TO ASK FOR WHEN TAKING A BOOKING
- RESPONDING TO BOOKINGS
- LAST-MINUTE BOOKINGS
- CREDIT CARDS OR CHEQUES?

along the route. Remember, guests may arrive late in the day or in winter and anything that helps them find you will be welcomed. Rather than specific mile distances from a junction, the advice 'turn right at the Crown Pub', or 'left at the post office' can be easier to follow. What may appear an easy route to you may be complicated to a first-time visitor, so don't feel you have to direct your guests along the shortest route possible using back roads. Keep directions simple, even if it adds on a few extra miles.

It is not unusual for the owner not to be present on arrival. This will depend on where you live and how convenient it will be for you to be present at the time of arrival. If you do live alongside your self-catering property, then this should not present any problems for you, but if you live many miles away then you will need to think about the arrival procedure. This may include using the help of your cleaner or caretaker, or could involve having the key collected or picked up from a pre-arranged spot. The details of this will need to be communicated at this final stage of the booking.

LAST-MINUTE BOOKINGS

If an enquiry or a booking is made within a very short time of the actual holiday dates you may need to receive full and final payment before the start of the holiday.

CREDIT CARDS OR CHEQUES?

More and more people rely on and expect to use credit cards for transactions, especially for large amounts. Accepting credit cards will certainly be very convenient for your guests, but it will cost you in terms of renting machines and losing a percentage of each transaction. Weigh up the pros and cons of having a credit card machine and think about it carefully before deciding whether or not to have one. If you are operating a single unit this can be very costly and may prove unrealistic. The plus side is that a credit card transaction will be credited to your account in less time than it takes for a cheque to be cleared.

Next chapter

At this stage you should have considered how your property will be furnished and decorated and have your operating policy in place. You now need to start making decisions on how you are going to promote your business.

The next chapter looks at launching your operation and gives an explanation on how tourism is managed in England, useful tips on advertising, brochure design and websites and details on the National Quality Assessment Schemes.

Bookings

- RECORDING BOOKINGS

- INFORMATION TO ASK FOR WHEN TAKING A BOOKING

- RESPONDING TO BOOKINGS

- LAST-MINUTE BOOKINGS

- CREDIT CARDS OR CHEQUES?

Chapter 5
Launching your operation

Even while you are in the preparatory stages of renovation or decoration, you need to think about advertising. Advertising can be very costly and it is only when you are up and running that you will you be able to ascertain exactly how your guests found out about you and which advertising worked best. It would be foolish to spend a fortune on advertising now and you may be inclined to think it is not sensible to do any advertising at all at this early stage. But how do you make potential visitors aware that your establishment exists and will be open for business, albeit perhaps in six months time? Is there anyone in the tourism field that can help you?

Tourism organisations

If you are considering starting a self-catering business then you may think that the first stop for advice would be the 'Tourist Board'. It is often assumed that there is just one national organisation that looks after tourism. That is not the case. There are in fact many organisations involved in promoting tourism and helping the industry. The many organisations vary in size from national to regional to local, but all work closely together.

HOW IS TOURISM MANAGED IN ENGLAND?

The national tourism organisation in the UK is VisitBritain (VB). It has an integral arm in England known as England Marketing working in the home and overseas markets. VB also works in conjunction with the Wales Tourist Board, Visit Scotland and the Northern Ireland Tourist Board. Its principal remit is to promote Britain, but it also promotes and helps develop quality (the NQAS), and carries out some research in support of those functions in England.

The responsibility for regional tourism rests with England's Regional Development Agencies (RDA). Each agency has a tourism section within its own structure or a sister organisation that it works with – the pattern varies a little region by region. The different regions of England work in slightly different ways and each has its own priorities dependent upon the nature of tourism in their particular region.

Your first stop should be with your local Tourist Information Centre (TIC). They are usually operated by your local authority and may, in turn, direct you to a regional Tourism Officer for more advice, or to the RDA's tourism department or Regional Tourist Board. Note that not every region in England has a Regional Tourist Board. Many are now part of their RDA.

While all of these different organisations work well, there is no one body in overall control of tourism in England. The best advice is to start locally.

ACCOMMODATION GUIDES

VisitBritain and many local authorities produce annual accommodation guides and these are also linked to their websites. In order that you can advertise with these organisations, you need to have your property assessed under the National Quality Assurance Schemes (NQAS). VisitBritain's Quality Assurance Schemes provide assurance to visitors that the advertised accommodation is meeting a recognised national standard and give an indication of the level of quality to expect.

All publications have lead times before printing. This is applicable to the major guidebooks such as VisitBritain's *Where to Stay* series and your local accommodation brochures and guides. The lead times will vary, but for the larger guides it can be five months before publication date. So if you miss the deadline, you will not be able to promote your property for another year.

Tourism organisations
– HOW IS TOURISM MANAGED IN ENGLAND?
– ACCOMMODATION GUIDES
– OTHER PUBLICATIONS

But if your property is not ready yet, you may wonder how can you be included in these guides? Provided that you have paid for an assessment, you will be eligible to have details of your accommodation included in the listing. Beside your entry in the guide, instead of a rating, will be the words 'applied for' or 'awaiting assessment', or similar. This clearly shows to any prospective visitor that you intend to become assessed and rated. If you are confident of your opening date, you could even include that information.

As a participant in VisitBritain's Quality Assurance Schemes you receive a free entry in the *Where to Stay* guide and a free listing on the website www.visitbritain.com, the official tourism website for Britain. Being quality assessed is also usually a condition that allows you an entry in regional guides and local accommodation guides. Produced by local authorities or regional tourism bodies they cover specific areas and there are usually associated costs. You may also consider advertising in paid-for guides.

OTHER PUBLICATIONS

Selecting other publications in which to advertise will require some market research. Go to a reference library and look at one of the national media guides such as *Willing's* or *Benn's*. These list all magazines and newspapers along with their circulation figures and will give you an idea of the range of publications available, and might help you to narrow the choice of where to advertise.

Depending on your location and your target market you could consider advertising in specialist magazines. For example, if you are aiming to attract specific markets, such as walkers, cyclists or birdwatchers, you may want to take out a small advert in a relevant publication. There will be numerous magazines available, so buy some copies and look through the adverts to see if other self-catering properties advertise. Publications are always keen to obtain advertising and in return might be able to provide you with the 'profile' of their readers. This will be invaluable in knowing if you are reaching the correct market and you will be able to judge whether these are the right publications for you, but be aware that advertising rates can vary greatly between different publications.

Also, be aware that a downside of any advertising is that you may be contacted by numerous other publications, such as other magazines and newspapers trying to persuade you to advertise with them. At this early stage in your business it will probably be more cost-effective to be selective with your advertising budget.

Developing a brochure

It is vital that you have a piece of print to send out to any enquiries that you receive. However, in the very early stages of developing your property it can prove expensive to produce a full-colour brochure. In addition, you may not be able to photograph your rooms or facilities as they are still in the process of being decorated and equipped. So what should you do?

INITIAL BROCHURE

In the interim you could consider producing a brochure yourself, using a personal computer, or have a line drawing produced by a local artist and use a high street printers to run off copies. This can be very effective and achieved for a relatively low cost.

Alternatively, you could choose to hand everything over to an agency. They can handle all the advertising and marketing, although their rates will vary and could be as much as 28% plus, per booking. As with everything there will be pros and cons. There is more advice on agencies in Chapter 9.

SUBSEQUENT BROCHURES

As the property is completed and costs become more affordable, you could consider a more professional brochure. You will need to consider carefully what information to include and how the brochure will be used.

A good first step is to do your own research. As detailed in Chapter 2, if you have contacted other self-catering properties, you may now have a small collection of brochures to study. If not, then do this next. When you have received a few lay them out on a table and look at them. What stands out, which is most appealing, which entices you to make a booking? Designing an effective brochure is not easy, but there are some simple tips to get it right. Consider from the assortment you have collected how well the design works and the layout, how easy are they to read, is there sufficient information about the property and are there any photographs? Would they make you want to go and stay there?

THE SIZE OF THE BROCHURE

When deciding on the size of the brochure it is worth considering how it will be used. Many brochures are sent in the post in response to requests for information. As such, the brochure needs to fit into an envelope and the most suitable sized envelope is a DL (11cm x 22cm) sized envelope. These take a single sheet of A4 paper folded into three. By designing your brochure as a three-fold A4 sheet, you will not need to buy special envelopes. In addition, you can post out complementary material to guests, such as local events and attractions leaflets. These are often produced in the same format.

THE FRONT COVER

The front cover is all important in providing a strong first impression of your property. Consider designing it with one simple image, which captures the property in the best light. If taking photographs yourself, use the early or late day sun to add warmth and shadows. Don't be afraid of taking pictures on cloudy days. A few clouds can add character and interest. You could also select a feature for the main photograph – a planted tub or hanging basket or the entrance door may all convey the right image for you.

The most important piece of information will be the property name; does it have one, or do you need to think of one? Names can be important and can be used as a marketing tool. If you are thinking of a fresh name for your property, try to think what impression it could convey. 'Hill View', for example, can create an image of a countryside location. 'The Old Rectory' may be exactly what your property is or

'Lavender Cottage' may refer to planting in the garden. A name, however, will always be easier for the visitor to remember than a street address.

The cover could also contain the location and contact details with e-mail and website, if applicable.

THE INTERIOR SPREAD

The interior of the brochure should not be too cluttered with information or just full of text. People want to know the main facts about the property, such as the size and number of rooms, but consider using pictures to sell the property, rather than too much text. You will need to have a description, but try to be accurate without being gushing with descriptions. Your definition of a 'luxurious, top-quality accommodation' may not match someone else's. Consider using floor plans to helpfully illustrate the overall size and layout of the property.

Internal pictures can be carefully staged to best reflect your accommodation. For example, if your property is in a rural area, which may appeal to birdwatchers, then a photograph of the lounge may be improved with the coffee table set with a bird book, pair of binoculars and an OS map. The bedroom may be best depicted if lights are on (indoor lighting can add warmth to a photograph) and the dining room could be set with plates, tablecloth and a vase of flowers, as if you are about to serve dinner. You could even show your welcome tray, complete with a bottle of wine on the table (if appropriate).

Highlight any special features, such as an inglenook fireplace, landscaped garden or the view from the bedroom window. Consider also highlighting any features that could affect visitors, such as a steep and narrow staircase to the bedroom.

Remember the outside, especially if you have a patio or decked area, with views, or a play area for children. And don't forget to list any policies, as regards pets, smoking and children, or any extras, such as fishing permits, included in the rate.

Developing a brochure

- INITIAL BROCHURE
- SUBSEQUENT BROCHURES
- THE SIZE OF THE BROCHURE
- THE FRONT COVER
- THE INTERIOR SPREAD
- THE REAR PANEL
- THE TARIFF

THE REAR PANEL

The rear panel is a very suitable place to put your location and contact details. Include simple, easy-to-follow directions and a location map. You could even consider a detailed location map and more general locator map of the region to show your proximity to the coast, places of interest or main towns and roads.

Another good idea is to identify distances from places of interest. Being just off a major road may appeal to some travellers, but proximity to a tourist attraction may be a draw for others. 'Just a 5-minute drive from the coast' or 'convenient city centre location' can all be used to good effect.

THE TARIFF

Whilst it is important to include details of your tariff, by printing your prices in your brochure you will be severely limiting its shelf life. Instead, consider printing the tariff on a separate insert. Even though this will involve additional costs, it can save amending old brochures and will enhance efficiency. The tariff sheet can also include details on how to make a booking.

Developing a website

The Internet is an increasingly important place for people looking for accommodation, and it will often be the first point of research for prospective guests.

THE IMPORTANCE OF WEBSITES

When on a website, guests will want to see pictures of the accommodation, gain information on rates, and possibly e-mail you with an enquiry. This allows them to make a more informed decision on where to stay, and to book their accommodation with greater ease. The Internet also allows guests to view details of many properties at once, as opposed to making individual phone enquiries and waiting for brochures to arrive.

SETTING UP A WEBSITE

You may be able to set up your own site. Alternatively, you could use a web designer. Whilst this will be more costly, the result may be a more professional-looking site, with greater ease of use and special features, such as 360 degree views of the property.

The great benefit of having a website is that it can be updated almost immediately and you will be able to have photographs of the accommodation added as they become ready. Consider adding photographs of the general area as well as of the accommodation. Although you are selling the accommodation in the first instance, you are also selling your location.

Obtaining your grading

Now that you have decided how to plan your self-catering property, finalised the overall design and content and have begun thinking about promoting your property, you next need to consider being assessed and graded. This section describes how VisitBritain's Quality Assurance Schemes operate and how the assessment is carried out.

THE NATIONAL QUALITY ASSURANCE SCHEME (NQAS)

In order for you to promote your property in any of the publications produced by VisitBritain and many local authorities and tourism organisations, you will need to have been awarded a quality rating. Being quality assessed is a very positive and constructive exercise, providing you with a lot of helpful and important advice at an early stage, as well as the marketing opportunities that only VisitBritain can offer.

The only organisation to operate a national grading scheme of self-catering properties in England is VisitBritain. This scheme is consistent throughout England, Scotland and Wales.

WHAT ARE THE BENEFITS OF BEING ASSESSED?

There are two main benefits from being assessed by VB. These could be referred to as the marketing benefits and the management benefits.

The marketing benefits include being able to show a quality rating alongside your business. It is an official and independent endorsement from the official tourism body for Britain. A rating provides your customers with the reassurance that you are meeting and maintaining quality standards. You can use the quality rating on your brochures, websites, any advertising you do, and on signage and stationery.

In addition, your property receives a free listing in the *Where to Stay* guides, the national guides for accommodation in England, and on VisitBritain's website. This listing is available to over 560 Tourist Information Centres in England, each of which receives hundreds of enquiries each day. Additionally, the listing is provided to all VB offices overseas.

The management benefits are the expert advice you receive from one of VisitBritain's quality assessors. Each assessor sees in excess of 300 accommodation operations a year and can offer advice on developing your property. The advice is suggestive and not prescriptive, that is, you don't have to take actions if you don't want to. The assessor's role is to assess where your operation sits with regard to a national rating. However, they are also there to discuss ideas and make suggestions based on what they have seen and experienced at other properties. The assessment becomes a very effective way of sharing best practice.

HOW DO YOU OBTAIN A RATING?

To achieve a rating you will first need to contact Quality in Tourism (details in Sources of further help) who carry out assessments on behalf of VisitBritain. There will be a fee, which is based on the number of units you have.

The assessment should take place within about six to eight weeks of Quality In Tourism acknowledging your application. In this time the assessor will be assigned the visit, and they will contact you to make an appointment for the assessment.

The assessor visits your property at a mutually convenient time. This will often be when the unit is not occupied, but not all visits can take place out of season and so inevitably, and if not too inconvenient, may be arranged for when it is occupied.

During the visit they will spend time explaining how the scheme operates, how quality is assessed and how grades are applied. They will then look round the property, usually accompanied by yourself or your agent, and look at all areas guests use during their stay. This will include the living areas, kitchen and dining room and the bedrooms and bathrooms, as well as the exterior of the property and surrounding grounds and gardens.

Their role is twofold: firstly to ensure you get the right grading for your property, and secondly, to provide advice and tips on developing quality. These latter points are really 'could do' ideas, not 'must do' action points. The only things you must do after any assessment is meet minimum standards. Should you not meet any of the minimum standards, these will be part of a written report for you to action before the next assessment.

After the visit you will receive confirmation of the grade achieved, the written quality assessment report and a certificate.

WHO ASSESSES AND WHAT ARE THEY LOOKING FOR?

Assessors come from an industry background to ensure they have an understanding and empathy with the tourism industry and understand guests' expectations. They undertake comprehensive training, which includes an annual seminar and individual one-to-one accompanied training. Throughout the year they receive further accompanied assessments. The detailed training programme helps to ensure that assessors are all working to the same objective standards.

All self-catering properties are graded from 1 to 5 stars. The requirements for minimum standards must be met by all properties. Minimum standards relate to the basic requirements for facilities and services. They cover aspects including cleanliness and being fit for purpose as well as, for example, having lights, providing a bath mat in the bathroom and ensuring there is a good range of crockery available. As quality standards increase beyond a minimum level, so the star rating will increase. Establishments at higher rating levels also have to meet some additional requirements for facilities.

Obtaining your grading

- THE NATIONAL QUALITY ASSURANCE SCHEME (NQAS)

- WHAT ARE THE BENEFITS OF BEING ASSESSED?

- HOW DO YOU OBTAIN A RATING?

- WHO ASSESSES AND WHAT ARE THEY LOOKING FOR?

- HOW DO THE FIVE RATINGS DIFFER?

The standards booklet for self-catering details all the minimum requirements for the National Quality Assurance Schemes. To get a copy of the booklet contact Quality in Tourism (see Sources of futher help).

HOW DO THE FIVE RATINGS DIFFER?

The following only provide an indication of the five star levels; relevant NQAS standards booklet will provide more comprehensive information.

One star

At one star the accommodation may be more simply decorated and furnished, although all areas will be safe and clean with the accommodation cleaned for visitors' arrival. The unit may not be self-contained and may have use of a shared bathroom. All equipment provided will work properly and be fit for its purpose and beds will be of at least standard adult size (unless advertised otherwise) and provided with clean bedding in sufficient quantity, although linen may, or may not, be provided.

Potential visitors will be given advance details of the accommodation, facilities and services available and all Health and Safety and Statutory obligations will be complied with.

Two stars

At two stars all units will be self-contained. Generally, there will be a good overall quality of décor, furnishings and fixtures, although these may be of a more practical or older style. Space may be limited, particularly in bedrooms and there will be at least one bathroom and WC for up to eight guests.

Three stars

The quality of décor and furnishings will demonstrate greater attention to coordination and practicality than at the previous two star levels. Accommodation will be more spacious, offering greater levels of comfort and greater freedom of movement. For example, there will be access to both sides of double beds. There will be good lighting arrangements throughout the property, and a bedside table and lamp for each occupant. Heating will be controllable and a wider range of appliances, including a microwave oven and vacuum cleaner, will be provided or available. At this star level there may be some leisure facilities, such as boxed games, toys and a barbecue, as appropriate.

Obtaining your grading

- THE NATIONAL QUALITY ASSURANCE SCHEME (NQAS)

- WHAT ARE THE BENEFITS OF BEING ASSESSED?

- HOW DO YOU OBTAIN A RATING?

- WHO ASSESSES AND WHAT ARE THEY LOOKING FOR?

- HOW DO THE FIVE RATINGS DIFFER?

Four stars

At four stars, accommodation is very comfortable. The property will be decorated to a high standard and there will be more space and more good quality furniture, soft furnishings, beds and floorings than at the previous three star levels. Bed linen and towels will be provided, with or without an additional charge. In the kitchen there will be a more extensive range of appliances, including access to a washing machine and tumble dryer (or the provision of a 24-hour laundry service). If more than six guests can be accommodated there will be an additional separate WC.

Five stars

At five stars accommodation is of an excellent quality. A high specification will be evident in all areas of the property, from the beds to flooring. There will be attention to detail evident in design, both internal and external, with exemplary standards of care and maintenance. Sleeping will be in designated bedrooms only; there will be no sofa beds.

A full range of appliances and equipment will be provided, including a freezer, dishwasher, in-house laundry facilities (or a 24-hour laundry service) and a telephone capable of receiving incoming and making outgoing calls.

Bed linen and towels will be available and included within the hire change. If more than six guests can be accommodated, an extra bath or shower, WC and washbasin will be provided.

Where leisure facilities are provided, these will be in excellent order, under supervision, where appropriate, and with extended opening hours to suit customer needs.

The management of the unit or organisation and levels of guest care will be exemplary.

Next chapter

In the next two chapters, we examine the guest journey from arrival to departure. We will look at arrival procedures and ideas to enhance first impressions, whether you are able to meet your guests or not, and the quality of the guest stay including information provision and ideas for extras that help exceed expectations.

Chapter 6
The arrival

'High quality is seldom achieved by chance. It is almost invariably the outcome of care, attention to detail, a fitness for the purpose intended allied to a genuine concern for the needs, comfort and convenience of the user.'

Welcome and arrival procedure

Unless you have decided to ask an agency to manage your property you need to consider what happens when your guests arrive. If you live some distance away you may have employed a caretaker to look after the cleaning and maintenance of your property, but will that person also be able to meet guests? If you live nearby, will you be able to meet them or will you have to leave the key for them to collect on arrival?

THE IMPORTANCE OF WELCOMING GUESTS

The preparation you make for your guests' arrival can be crucial to their enjoyment of the property and their holiday. Many people will have travelled a long distance, some will have young children who may be fretful, whilst others may have encountered traffic delays. If you are unable to provide a personal welcome you might be tempted to just leave the front door key under the doormat or in a specified place. On entering the property your guests may then have to hunt around to find light switches, work out for themselves how to operate the heating and hot water and then start making the beds. And all of that before they have been able to unpack and unwind. It may not be the best start to a holiday.

Conversely, consider if on arrival you are there to meet them but are in a hurry yourself. You rush them through the property, quickly showing them the various rooms and impart lots of information to them, fire lots of questions at them, and then disappear leaving them to look after themselves. Again, this may not be the best start to a holiday. The objective with your arrival procedure should be to achieve the best first impression whether you are there or not and the right balance between leaving your guests entirely to their own devices and being a burden when all they want to do is settle in and relax.

ARRIVAL PROCEDURE IF YOU CANNOT MEET GUESTS ON ARRIVAL

How will your guests gain entry if there is no one to meet them? If keys have to be collected from a different location, such as a village shop, what will happen if they are delayed? Will there be a suitable alternative?

Consider leaving the door unlocked (or if not appropriate, leave the key in an easy-to-find location), and prepare the property for their arrival. If you cannot arrange for your guests to be met on arrival, then consider what a difference and how much more welcoming it will be if you can arrange for something personal to welcome them. Consider preparing a tea tray. This is done in many self-catering properties, and can be left with biscuits and a welcome card. The card can be personalised and can include the suggestion that they contact you if they have any problems.

If there is a telephone in the property you could even consider calling them on the first evening just to check they have settled in comfortably. If close by, you could also suggest they call you on arrival so you can come round and explain how everything works.

ARRIVAL PROCEDURE IF YOU CAN MEET GUESTS ON ARRIVAL

It is a good idea to find out when your guests plan to arrive. As most people have mobile phones, providing there is reception, you could even suggest they ring you at an agreed time, for example, two hours before their arrival. This will allow you to get the property fully prepared and be at the property to meet them.

Once they arrive, highlight any really important points, such as the heating controls, and answer any of their immediate concerns. Then leave them. They may be tired after a long journey, want a hot drink or need to use the facilities. Suggest that they contact you if there are any queries, but allow them to settle in at their own pace. If you have to arrange for someone else to be there for their arrival, it can be a consideration to drop by after a day or so and introduce yourself, although you would need to judge if this is appropriate or not. Personal contact can make such a difference and may avert any potential problems or complaints. If something is faulty, it will give you the opportunity to take remedial action, rather than hearing about it on the day they leave.

If you live far away and employ a caretaker, you will have to try and find an acceptable balance that suits you both and yet offers a good welcome for your guests. Although it may not be possible for a caretaker to be on hand when they arrive, hopefully they will be able to prepare the property ready for the guests' arrival.

Preparations for arrival

How exactly should you prepare your guests for arrival and how should you prepare the property? What needs to be done? What would your guests expect? And, what can make the best first impression?

PREPARING YOUR GUESTS

You will have already mailed information on the booking to your guests, including a map and directions. Advise them also of parking arrangements. If you do not have off-road parking, ensure they are aware of where they can safely park, both for unloading their vehicle on arrival and for the duration of their stay.

FIRST IMPRESSIONS

You never have a second opportunity to make a first impression. First impressions are vital in starting your guests off on the right footing and ensuring they are happy with their stay. A poor first impression can often result in a guest finding fault with other aspects of their stay. Very often a complaint about a stay in a self-catering property is based

---

Welcome and arrival procedure

- THE IMPORTANCE OF WELCOMING GUESTS
- ARRIVAL PROCEDURE IF YOU CANNOT MEET GUESTS ON ARRIVAL
- ARRIVAL PROCEDURE IF YOU CAN MEET GUESTS ON ARRIVAL

Preparations for arrival

- PREPARING YOUR GUESTS
- FIRST IMPRESSIONS
- SIGNAGE AND LIGHTING
- PARKING
- DO GUESTS KNOW WHERE TO GO ON ARRIVAL?
- GARDENS

on a poor first impression – after which everything else seems to go wrong.

For some guests, first impressions may start with their telephone enquiry, but their true first impressions will start on arrival. Whether you are in a busy city centre, a sea-front esplanade or tucked away in a rural location, you want guests to arrive in a pleasant frame of mind. You could suggest that creating a pleasant frame of mind is out of your control, but it does start with finding your property and finding it with ease.

SIGNAGE AND LIGHTING

You may or may not have exterior signs. Not every property has signs to advertise itself, but you should have something that identifies you as the self-catering property your guests have booked. Be aware that some signs may require planning permission, and if you do have signage, even if just a house name, consider if it is clear and well lit. Can your guests see it at night as well as in the daytime? At multi-unit properties you will need names or numbers for each unit. Consider placing these by the entrance door and near exterior lights so they are easily seen at night.

For guests arriving in daylight, finding your property may be relatively straightforward. But what if they are arriving after dark and in the rain? Some properties avoid prominent signage because they want to retain a low profile and not upset the neighbours. In these instances they often have a nameplate that is easy to see, or an unusual feature (such as a white-painted milk churn at a farmhouse property) to identify their entrance. One of the easiest signs to spot can be that of your quality assurance rating.

You should also consider whether there is sufficient lighting around your property for guests when they arrive and during their stay. Exterior lighting is very important. Ensure there is lighting above or by the front door. Consider having sensor lighting to highlight the door, parking areas and the route from their car to your entrance door. If you install sensor lighting, think carefully about where you site it. It needs to be effective for guests when arriving and unloading their cars. Remember, guests unloading their car will take longer than you unloading the shopping. The lighting may need to be on longer than would be normal to accommodate their needs.

PARKING

Convenient parking is an important consideration for many guests. When arriving at a self-catering property guests will need to unpack their cars. They will tend to bring much more than if staying away in a B&B or a hotel. Consider if they arrive during bad weather. Will they be able to unload easily and can they park adjacent to the property?

If you have space for off-road parking, is it immediately obvious where guests can park their car? You may want to consider small but obvious signage indicating 'guest parking', especially if you have a multi-unit site, where you may have a number of vehicles parked. If the driveway is gated, consider leaving the gate open for their arrival. This can be especially helpful in bad weather.

If it is necessary for guests to park on the roadside, advise them on where to park and check their location so that their vehicle does not inconvenience neighbours. If your self-catering property is on a farm or if another business operates from your home, you may need to make it evident where guests should park, to avoid other traffic.

DO GUESTS KNOW WHERE TO GO ON ARRIVAL?

This may seem like an unusual question, but at some properties the front door is not obvious. You may have a property with two entrance doors, one of which is no longer used and blocked up and the main entrance used is the former kitchen door. You know this, but does the guest arriving for the very first time?

A very useful technique is to frame the front door to make it obvious from a distance. You can use planters, hanging baskets and lighting all to good effect. You do not need a sign that says 'entrance', but you do need to make the entrance obvious.

If you have a multi-unit site then you will want to meet your guests as they arrive to direct them to their unit. Be prepared for their arrival, possibly meet them outside as they get out of their car and show them where to park to unload and, if different, where to park for the duration of their stay. If you have a gravel driveway, you should hear them when they do arrive. Otherwise, be sure to ask them for an expected time of arrival.

GARDENS

If you have gardens and grounds then it obviously helps to keep them neat and tidy. Weeds and unkempt bushes or broken gutters and damaged external decoration will not help to create that positive first impression. Year-round external maintenance is important. If you have little or no garden, then you can still introduce colour with hanging baskets, or wall-fixed planters where appropriate, to add character to the property. Any outdoor furniture or barbecues will need to be in good condition and any play equipment neatly stored away. If you accept pets, you may need to be extra vigilant in keeping the garden clean and tidy.

Preparing the property

Carefully preparing the property for your guests can make a very strong first impression. This is one of the most important aspects of managing your property. It ensures guests' needs are not only met but exceeded and, as the definition of quality at the beginning of this chapter states, illustrates 'a genuine concern for the needs, comfort and convenience of the user'.

ATTENTION TO DETAIL

Little touches go a long way. Ensure that the hot water is on for your guests' arrival, so they do not have to switch an immersion heater or a boiler on and wait for hot water. Depending on the time of the year, consider putting the heating on or adjust the timer accordingly. The beds should all be made up (if linen is provided) and towels placed out ready for use.

For guests arriving after dark or on a cold winter evening, consider how much more pleasant it would be if the curtains were drawn and light and heating switched on. You need not put all the lights on, but a few table lamps will set the right ambience and provide sufficient illumination for your guests as they enter. It will also add warmth.

TEA TRAYS AND WELCOME BASKETS

Preparing a tea tray can be done whether or not you are able to meet your guests. Leave the tray in the kitchen and prepare it ready to make that first cup of tea or coffee. Leave sufficient cups for the number of guests arriving, sugar, tea and coffee, and leave the kettle empty but the lid open to indicate it needs to be filled.

In addition to the basics you could also leave a welcome basket. A bowl of fruit, half a dozen local free-range eggs, a small loaf of bread, a bottle of mineral water, a small packet of biscuits, individually wrapped portions of cake or chocolate, or a plate of homemade shortbread, a pint of fresh milk in the fridge, a bottle of wine and a carton of orange juice for the children. If practical, add fresh flowers. The appearance and the smell can make a big difference to first impressions. Place a welcome card by the basket. It will be noticed as soon as your guests arrive and adds a personalised touch.

For any repeat guests you could leave a more personal welcome card and, if you are aware from any correspondence or telephone conversations that there is a birthday or anniversary, then chocolates or wine might be a good consideration. For Christmas and New Year a decorated tree could even be a good, personal touch.

All of these touches will enhance your guests' first impressions. You will need to cover your costs within the rental of the property, but setting up a tea tray, putting together a welcome basket and arranging some cut flowers in a vase need not cost you much. Decide what is practical and what is not, but do provide something. It will make a difference.

Preparations for arrival

- PREPARING YOUR GUESTS
- FIRST IMPRESSIONS
- SIGNAGE AND LIGHTING
- PARKING
- DO GUESTS KNOW WHERE TO GO ON ARRIVAL?
- GARDENS

Preparing the property

- ATTENTION TO DETAIL
- TEA TRAYS AND WELCOME BASKETS
- ESSENTIALS NOT EXTRAS

ESSENTIALS NOT EXTRAS

There are some items that are more essential for your guests. In the kitchen consider leaving a small supply of tea, coffee and sugar, washing-up liquid, dishwasher tablets and bin liners. In the bathroom provide soap and toilet rolls. You will need to leave a small selection of general cleaning materials, such as cloths and cream cleaners, and these will also encourage your guests to maintain your standards of housekeeping. If you have an open fire or a wood burning stove, a few logs, coal, kindling or firelighters will be helpful. These small items can make a lot of difference to your guests' first impressions.

Case study
Unit preparation

Our self-catering property is a barn conversion that can accommodate up to six people. Fortunately, we live on site which means that we can be here when guests arrive. In deciding what to provide as a welcome for our guests, we each made a list of what we had been given in holiday homes that we had been to, and added to this things we would like to find. Naturally our lists differed greatly – his included a bottle of red wine and a local newspaper, whereas I thought fresh milk and a tea tray with cake or biscuits would be more important.

We eventually reached agreement and now leave a pre-set tea tray and a welcome basket. There's a pint of milk in the fridge plus a small starter pack of teabags with a small jar of coffee and one of sugar. I also provide a small pot of local honey, six free-range eggs and some fruit. We decided against the wine, apart from at Christmas and Easter, as a decent bottle for every booking would have been a bit expensive. However, I always leave a vase of fresh flowers. The smell really makes a difference.

In advance of their arrival I double-check that the hot water is switched on, and if they are arriving late in the

---

evening, leave the curtains drawn, a few table lights on and the outside light on. The beds are always made up and I leave cleaning cloths, tablets for the dishwasher, a few bin bags and tea towels in the kitchen and always plenty of toilet tissue in the bathroom.

When guests arrive, one of us will go out to meet them. We realized very early on that this works best but also that they tend to want to settle in very quickly. They are given a very brief tour of the property, in particular, highlighting the location of heating and hot water controls. Naturally we answer any of their queries, but then after ensuring they are aware of the information folders, they are left to settle in. We always offer to call in the next day to see if there are any problems, but leave it open for them to decide.

As we live close by there could be the temptation to keep 'dropping in' but we never do. Obviously, we wave and chat in passing, but we always leave them to have a relaxed holiday and hope that they will want to return. They usually do!

Preparing the property

- ATTENTION TO DETAIL
- TEA TRAYS AND WELCOME BASKETS
- ESSENTIALS NOT EXTRAS

Next chapter

In the next chapter we look at the guests' stay and ideas to enhance the quality of that stay. We focus on information that you can provide to help them plan their stay, whether they are working in the area or they are on holiday.

Chapter 7
Catering for themselves

How can you make your guests' stay that extra bit special?

They will almost certainly have chosen to stay in your property because of its location and may already have planned some of their leisure time. Many will have carried out research as to what there is to see and do, whilst others will have rushed away from a busy life without too much preparation. Although you will never know what your guests' exact interests are, you can, without too much hard work, put together some information that will help them get the most from their stay. You are ultimately hoping to generate repeat visits, and by whetting their appetite for the area, you will hopefully encourage them to return, not to mention telling others about the area and your property.

Property information

In all self-catering properties you need to provide comprehensive information on the property and how to get help in case of an emergency. Although you may have met your guests on arrival, you may have only had a very short time to advise them of any important issues. To not only help them to have an enjoyable holiday, but also to avoid any unnecessary calls for assistance, you need to provide additional information.

Property information

- INFORMATION FOLDER
- INFORMATION TO INCLUDE
- ADDITIONAL INFORMATION

INFORMATION FOLDER

The best way to present any additional information is in an information folder. The NQAS standards booklet for the self-catering scheme details all the essential information you need to provide and will help you to prepare your property for lettings. Bear in mind that whilst the worst case scenario will probably never happen, it is sensible to be prepared for various situations, just in case.

INFORMATION TO INCLUDE

The list below includes the essential information that you should provide:

- Your name, address and telephone numbers, or those of your agent or caretaker – if there is an emergency, if there is a leak from a water pipe, or the oven fails to work, your guests will need help. This will obviously need to include daytime, mobile and evening numbers.
- The telephone number of the property and whether incoming calls can be received – not all self-catering properties have a telephone, but if there is one, do show the number clearly and identify if the guest can receive calls as well making outgoing calls. This is important in case your guests are needed in the case of a family emergency.
- The location of the nearest public telephone – this is very useful if you neither have a telephone in the property or cannot receive a strong mobile telephone signal in your area. Although your guests have come away on a break, they may need to keep in touch with friends and family.
- The address and telephone numbers of emergency services including the local doctor, A&E hospital, local police station, dentist and, if applicable, vet – emergency situations are very rare indeed, but should an unfortunate accident occur you need to have this information clearly displayed for guests to get help. Consider having an

information board somewhere conveniently located, such as in the entrance hall or in the kitchen, with this and your own contact details posted.

- The location of the stopcock and fuse box – you don't really want guests touching fuse boxes or turning off the water supply, but in an emergency it may be necessary.
- Instructions for operating the heating and hot water – this will be essential, as all guests will need to know how to operate these. You may have a system set by a timer to operate the hot water in the early morning and again in the evening, and the same for the central heating. However, if guests need to change the system or boost the water or heating for an hour, make sure they know how to do so.
- Relevant warnings about sceptic tanks or macerator WCs – this will only apply to some properties, but where you do have such systems, guests need to be aware and advised accordingly about what can be flushed and what needs to be binned. It will also save you the expense of getting things fixed, and avoid inconvenienced guests.
- Details of where spare bulbs, torch and spare fuses are kept – bulbs and fuses may blow and torches may be needed in a power cut. Keep all items easily to hand and make guests aware at the start of their stay where they are.
- The location of the fire blanket or extinguisher – these must be prominently displayed.
- Details on refuse and recycling collection days and whether any specific bins, boxes or bags have to be used – this is very useful information. If your refuse collection is on a Thursday but changeover day is Saturday, your new guests will not want bins full of rubbish sitting outside for most of their week. This advice may not be used by all guests, but will prove useful for most.
- The location of the nearest recycling facilities and bottle bank – as above, not all guests will worry about this aspect, and indeed, it may be easier and more convenient for you to deal with all recycling. However, some guests will be grateful for this information and will act upon it.

- Operating instructions for any kitchen equipment, such as the oven, dishwasher, washing machine, tumble dryer or water softener – all white goods vary and although most guests will be used to their own washing machine or oven, they may not know how to use yours. Providing these details will be especially useful if you have an AGA, combi-oven or dishwasher.
- Details of television channels – all guests should be aware of the terrestrial channels, but if you also have Freeview channels or satellite channels, list these as well and give instructions on how to use the remote controls. You could even add a copy of that week's TV guide.
- Operational instructions for the television, video or DVD and CD players – as with kitchen equipment, these may not be as obvious to use as you think. Leave the instruction manual for guests, just in case they have a problem.
- A copy of the Yellow Pages or local directory – guests may need a garage or want details of local restaurants or taxi firms and may find these very useful. If you know of any reputable local taxi firms you could add their card to the information board or place it in the information folder.

Property information

- INFORMATION FOLDER
- INFORMATION TO INCLUDE
- ADDITIONAL INFORMATION

ADDITIONAL INFORMATION

Another aspect that many guests will be interested in is the property itself. If you have converted a barn, renovated a house, constructed a new building or own an historic property, then consider putting together an information folder on what you achieved. Many owners of self-catering properties, which are conversions or renovations, compile a photo album charting the project for guests to see how the property was transformed. Date and caption the photos to add interest.

Any special information about your property, such as historical features, any interesting facts about a nearby village or if a nearby stately home was used for a TV series or film, could all help to make your guests' stay more enjoyable and more memorable.

Local information

- Guest information is an area where you can help to provide a distinctive stay and enhance the overall quality of the guest experience. Whether guests are staying because they are working or are on holiday, they may arrive in the area with little knowledge of what there is to see and do.

- You may think of other pieces of advice or information, relevant to your area that you could also include. Your knowledge of the area can be invaluable, and putting together information folders or having an information board can be very effective ways of imparting this knowledge to your guests.

- Information on shops – it can be very useful to list the location and opening times of a local food shop, in case guests run out of milk or need provisions on their first day. In addition, provide details on the nearest post office and chemist, as well as high street shops and shopping centres. If you live in an area where there is late-night shopping or half-day closing, give this information as well.

- Market days and the location of any farmers' markets – guests may welcome information on local markets, especially farmers' markets. You could also include information on car boot sales.

- Location of banks and building societies and the nearest cash point.

- Details of local public transport, including rail and bus timetables – for many guests, arriving by car is a necessity but being able to leave the car in the driveway and use public transport can both be welcomed and make life easier. Give details of any local bus routes and add advice on any park and ride schemes that may prove easier to use than negotiating city centre traffic. The location of the nearest cycle hire is also a consideration.

- Local hire shop for videos or DVDs – you may have an arrangement where your guests can use a local video shop and this could be useful for them during their stay.

- Details of local restaurants and pubs – although guests have booked self-catering, for many it is the need for a comfortable and spacious 'home from home' that made them book, not the desire to cook all week. Many guests will go out some nights, and having a selection of local menus from a variety of establishments will be very useful in helping them plan their week and enjoy themselves. You may have a local restaurant and eating out guide, or you could include menus ranging from a simple pub menu to cafés to more formal restaurants. You could even create a folder of local menus. If you do so, consider adding a blank page by each menu headed 'Guest's feedback' and leave it to your guests to make comments on each place.

- Location of takeaway restaurants and delivery services – include a selection of takeaway menus.

- Maps – a local map, OS map of the area or a bespoke map centred on your property, could all be very useful to identify your location relative to places of interest. This can be framed and hung on the wall as a very handy reference for guests. Around the map you could even place the leaflets of local attractions and indicate where each is, either with a number or by connecting the leaflet to its location with a length of thread. At some self-catering properties the same has been done for local eateries to show where each one is located and how to get there.

- Walking maps – you could put together a bespoke walking map from your property making use of your knowledge of local footpaths, country lanes and bridleways to create a short and a long walk; a 'red' and a 'blue' trail; a 20-minute stroll or an hour's walk. Depending on your location, you could even suggest a jogging route.

- Location of local churches, synagogues and mosques – this may not be required by all guests, but could be important and very useful information for some. If possible, you could also include service times.

- Local advice – the list of information you should and could provide can be endless, but you may want to include information specific to your location. For example, some coastal self-catering properties give details on boat trips to see seals, birdwatching sites and tide timetables to help guests plan their days.

Tourist information

With tourist information you can offer advice on a wide variety of days out and activities, from fun days at a theme park to watching seals from a desolate coast, to visiting a quirky museum or a grand historic house. It could be action-packed, cultural or just a leisurely lazy rest in a beautiful garden or nature reserve.

PRESENTING TOURIST INFORMATION

Instead of collecting a mass of tourist and visitor attraction leaflets and booklets from the local tourist information office and leaving them in a shoebox in a cupboard, or accumulating leaflets over many years and just dumping them all in a cupboard drawer, you could consider keeping leaflets and information neat and tidy and easy to use. You can do this in a variety of ways, but two you may consider are an information rack and tourist information folders.

INFORMATION RACKS

An information rack can be made by yourself or obtained from a leaflet distribution company. Contact your local tourist information centre for more advice on getting information racks. Racks allow you to keep leaflets neatly presented and you can theme the information in them. For example, you could have a main rack in the hallway of local places of interest, and a smaller leaflet holder in the living room with 'what's on' guides.

TOURIST INFORMATION FOLDERS

An alternative method of presenting the information is in a series of information folders, sectioned by topic. Using different coloured folders with plastic inserts you can easily add, remove and update information. However, you should make certain that folders are checked regularly as information can get removed, becomes out of date and can get dog-eared and worn – presentation is all important.

The following are five suggested themes for information folders. You may adopt some of these ideas if not all of them, depending on your operating style and the needs of your guests.

Local information

Tourist information

- PRESENTING TOURIST INFORMATION
- INFORMATION RACKS
- TOURIST INFORMATION FOLDERS
- OTHER INFORMATION

Folder 1 – Public transport

For guests who will only use public transport, including those who may have come by car and want a break from driving, you need to obtain details of all local means of transport, including taxi companies, train and bus timetables as well as coach tour operators who organise day excursions. Unless you are able to obtain a supply of the relevant timetables, you may need to photocopy originals. Remember to update these when seasonal changes come into effect. Coach operators will usually have a printed programme of planned excursions.

You could also include an approximate distance and time to get to various destinations. If visitor attractions are accessible by public transport include their leaflets, and for larger towns add details of tourist information centres. Visitors will be able to find additional suggestions from their offices, such as guided walking tours.

Folder 2 – Days out by car

This will be aimed towards those with their own means of transport and could include the main attractions as well as a selection of places that are off the beaten track. Divide the folder into sections to cover 'History and heritage' (including historic houses, monuments, museums and galleries), 'Family fun' (including animal and bird collections, amusement and theme parks, indoor play centres and leisure pools), 'Countryside' (covering cycling, walking, sailing, climbing, country parks and nature reserves, mills, boating and golf), 'Towns and cities' (including major annual events and festivals, market days, early closing, tourist information centres and guided tours) and 'Gardens' (covering gardens open for viewing, specialist nurseries, botanical gardens, arboretums, vineyards and water gardens). Include details of opening times, admission charges, parking, catering facilities, accessibility, tours, picnic sites and, if pertinent, whether dogs are allowed.

Folder 3 – Eating out

As highlighted above, a folder containing various menus from, for example, cafés, bistros, coffee shops, pubs, teashops, formal or family restaurants, can all be useful information for guests. Include menus with prices, if possible and opening hours. As mentioned previously, a page with recommendations from other guests and their comments can also be very useful.

Folder 4 – Days out itineraries

The idea of this folder is for you to personally compile a series of suggested itineraries for days out. These could highlight local places of interest and specify a suggested route between them, possibly using scenic roads or quieter lanes. Detail the road numbers and give clear directions, using visual aids wherever appropriate. Itineraries allow you to guide your guest around your area, pointing out historic churches, antique centres, local museums, historic houses and specialist shops, as well as places to eat. Always include parking locations and approximate distances between places and an overall duration.

The aim of the itinerary would be for visitors to return by a different route, so a circular tour could be very effective, and try to plan the itinerary to return before dark. You don't want to specify exact times for the day out, but you can suggest somewhere for morning coffee, a place for a light lunch and afternoon stop to give a suggestion of a timetable for the day.

Don't just do one itinerary but consider compiling a series to cover different themes, as in the 'Days out by car' folder.

Case study
A local touring itinerary for the guests

Detailed below is an example of a local touring itinerary based on a rural self-catering property, which guests holidaying the area could use if they choose. There have been examples of self-catering properties preparing a number of these and then printing off five from their PC and personalising them. For example,

---

'Mr and Mrs Smith – some ideas for a sunny day!' Each itinerary can have a theme, such as 'Interesting gardens', 'Historic houses and a good pub lunch', 'A steam railway and a riverside walk', 'A bird reserve with binoculars', 'Boating with a cream tea'. It takes some thought, but it can be done.

A DAY OUT FROM THE GRANGE

Take the A134 and drive 2 miles to Lavenham. The market place is in the centre of this medieval wool village where you will also find parking. From the Tourist Information Centre in Lady Street (just off the market place) you can hire an audio walking guide and, at your own pace, see the magnificent timber-framed buildings, Corpus Christi Guildhall (National Trust) and the glorious high-towered 16th-century church. There are plenty of galleries, interesting shops and a wide range of pubs, teashops and restaurants to visit enroute.

Leave Lavenham on the A1141 towards Sudbury and, after passing the church on the right, take the minor road signposted to Long Melford. The village is famous as the location for the filming of the *Lovejoy* TV series. The main street (1 mile) is the longest village street in England and has numerous antique shops. There are two historic houses here: Long Melford Hall (National Trust) and Kentwell Hall, a moated Elizabethan mansion which is renowned for its annual Tudor Recreations. Hidden away at the top of the village green is the beautiful Holy Trinity church.

Travel south on the A311 to Sudbury, birthplace of Thomas Gainsborough. A bronze statue of the artist is prominent in the market place, where you can also park and follow the signposts to Gainsborough's House. Now a museum and gallery it displays an amazing collection of his work. After a tour of the house you can relax in the walled garden and café.

Take the B1071 out of Sudbury and through the village of Boxford until you branch off towards Kersey, a picturesque village, famous for the water splash across the street. Look out for the ducks as you drive through it! At the top of the hill is yet another high-towered church – St Mary's. Leave on the minor road signposted towards Lavenham, only 6 miles away, but if you feel the need for a cream tea, call in enroute at Corncraft in Monks Eleigh.

Folder 5 – 'By foot or by pedal'

On a similar theme to the 'Days out by car' and the 'Days out itineraries', you could also compile a folder for days out by foot and bike. Include places to visit within a few hours' cycle from your property and of varied distances. This will cater for the needs of both the novice and the more experienced walker or cyclist. Like the car itineraries, include interesting places to stop and suitable pubs or cafés where someone walking or cycling could easily stop.

If you permit dogs, then include some suggested walks, but also detail any areas to avoid, such as lambing fields.

OTHER INFORMATION

Local tourist information does not just include tourist leaflets. It can also include local guidebooks and even information videos and DVDs. This will give your guests an opportunity to gain a general impression of the area. You might want to put a label on each of the book covers – '*Please do borrow this book during your stay but do remember to leave it behind for the enjoyment of other guests'*.

Guests' comment books

A guests' comment or suggestion book will give guests the opportunity to add their own comments about the area. This offers an opportunity for them to suggest places to visit, wildlife seen in the garden or advice on local eateries.

THE IMPORTANCE OF A GUEST BOOK

A guest book can be quite a useful tool. It involves the guest more closely with your property and area, encouraging them to record why and what they enjoyed about the stay.

This can promote a positive memory about the holiday. It also allows suggestions and recommendations to be made to other guests without any redress on you. If you advised someone to go to a particular pub for dinner and they had a bad experience, it may not reflect well on you. But if another guest does this, then it's more a case of their bad luck.

FEEDBACK FORMS

You could also consider providing a guest log book or feedback form. Unlike the comment book, this is mainly for your benefit. It provides an opportunity for the guest to tell you what worked, and perhaps what did not work so well for them. Was the heating too noisy, was the oven too difficult to operate and was there a draught from the front door? This is all useful and constructive feedback that guests may be happy to record on a form but be not so eager to give face to face.

Extras and accessories

Having prepared a series of itineraries, put together thematic tourist information folders and presented your collection of information leaflets tidily in racks, compiled your property information folder with equipment user guides and fixed your information board with emergency details, is there anything else that you can provide that can make your guests' stay even more enjoyable? In Chapter 3 we identified how to prepare your property and gave ideas on how to equip it. Below are some further ideas on extras that your guests could find useful.

OUTDOOR EXTRAS

Consider what your guests will be doing and where they will be going during their stay. If there are picnic spots nearby, could you leave a rug, flask, cooler bag, picnic plates and cutlery and folding chairs? Although guests may have brought a pre-stocked cooler bag with them, they may not have thought about or have had room to pack suitable seating. Large umbrellas and binoculars could be useful for the occasional walker. In the garden a sturdy and easy-to-operate sun parasol could be welcomed. Play equipment can help on sunny days, or if there are nearby tennis courts, consider providing some racquets and balls.

SITTING ROOM AND KITCHEN EXTRAS

In the sitting room consider adding a collection of paperbacks. Regularly check these for damaged pages, but add a small tent card on the bookshelf inviting guests to 'borrow' one and in return leave another. You'll soon start to accumulate new books.

In addition to books, consider providing some magazines. These could be local or regional publications giving a more in-depth insight into the area and featuring areas of specific interest.

If you provide a CD, video or DVD player, you could provide a few pre-recorded CDs, videos and DVDs. Consider also leaving a blank video for guest use. This could be very useful if they want to record their favourite soap and still go out for the evening. A radio is also very useful. You could provide one in the living room and one in the kitchen as well, if practical.

Boxed games and playing cards can provide great rainy day activities, but do check them every now and then to ensure pieces are not missing. Holidays are often the only time that families will play board games and if you do provide jigsaws think about a 'jigsaw roll' – it will mean that the dining table does not have to be cleared away before a meal is served. Depending on your guests, you could also provide pens or pencils and a notepad, if thought appropriate.

Extras such as coasters can be helpful. They may show local scenes and will avoid cup marks on your tables. You can also add a more personal touch with ornaments or framed pictures. However, avoid any family pictures otherwise you will over-personalise the accommodation.

In the kitchen, think about some recipe books and scales. You could provide some additional equipment such as a blender, juicer, coffee grinder or food processor (remember to leave operating instructions). A clock is a very helpful feature, and even if there is one on your oven, a larger, wall-mounted clock can be useful. You could even provide an egg timer. You'll be providing cloths, but also provide kitchen roll. And don't forget a first aid kit, though you'll need to check it regularly.

Extras and accessories

- OUTDOOR EXTRAS

- SITTING ROOM AND KITCHEN EXTRAS

- BEDROOM AND BATHROOM EXTRAS

BEDROOM AND BATHROOM EXTRAS

Consider the needs of your guests and provide those little extras that sometimes make all the difference. Consider those 'screaming subtleties' that can be highly effective but low cost.

Here is a list of some of the things that self-catering operators provide for their guests. Some of these you may like and want to adopt; some you may decide are not for you. And remember, you do not need to provide everything!

- Radio alarm clock – but remember to check the time and switch the alarm off on changeover day for new guests.
- Pot pourri sachets for the wardrobe and drawers – to add a fresh fragrance and avoid mustiness.
- Lining paper in drawers – to prevent splinters catching clothes.
- Hairdryer and clothes brush – both useful additions.
- Shoe cleaning kit – especially helpful if you have guests attending a wedding or smart event.
- Sewing kit – consider pre-threading some needles.
- Spare blankets and a hot water bottle.
- Plants or flowers – having something animate in a room can help to enhance its overall ambience and appearance.

In the bathroom you could include a range of toiletries, including soap, shampoo, bath and shower foam. If you choose to use large bottles ensure that these are kept topped up to maintain appearances.

Providing additional toiletries can also be very useful. You could consider a small basket of 'in-case-you-forgot' items. This could contain a travel toothbrush and toothpaste, a disposable razor, tissues, cotton wool, cotton buds, emery boards, sewing kit and a shower cap.

Next chapter

In the next chapter we look at the changeover day and assess efficient and effective ways of cleaning up after one set of guests, focusing on cleaning schedules, and preparing for the next.

Chapter 8
Changeover day

Changeover day needs to be managed efficiently and effectively. The day you choose will depend largely on the other self-catering properties in your area and also the type of guests you attract and what suits them. Whatever day you decide on you will need to ensure that your departing guests leave on time and that you have a well-organised routine in place to allow you to thoroughly freshen and clean your property, ready for your next visitors. Otherwise, you may find your new guests are anxiously sitting in the car outside wanting to get in and start their holiday while you are still cleaning!

Establishing a changeover routine

Changeover day has finally come but, as you wave goodbye to one set of guests, how do you ensure that your property will be ready for the next? In this section we look at the importance of setting up a changeover routine and developing checklists.

DECIDING ON YOUR CHANGEOVER DAY

Changeover day for the self-catering industry is traditionally Saturday. Most guests will want to start their holiday at the start of a weekend and stay away for a full week. It does happen that some self-catering operators operate different changeover days and you may want to do so yourself. Be aware though of the impact this may have on your bookings. It may be useful to check what other self-catering properties are doing in your area. If some do operate a different changeover day you may want to contact them to see how well it works for them. But if everyone operates on a Saturday changeover day, this may reflect market demands.

When deciding on the changeover day you will need to take into consideration a number of factors. If you are intending to employ a cleaner or a caretaker, perhaps because you live far away, you need to check that they are always available to work on a Saturday. If you decide to take short-break stays, then you will add another day to the 'usual' changeover day. There may also be the times when you let the property for a two-week stay. In this circumstance, you may offer to have it cleaned mid-way through their stay or, if not, will there be an excessive amount to do on the following week.

WHAT TO DO ON THE DAY

On changeover day, you or your cleaner or agent may have arrived at the property before your guests have left. Be specific about departure times in your terms and conditions, and whilst you may want to wish them a safe journey and hope that they return, spending a long time chatting will not only delay them but also put pressure on you to clean and prepare the property for the new arrivals.

Depending on your terms and conditions, you may need to take meter readings for electricity consumption and then sort out any due payment. Guests may also want to inform you about any problems during their stay or breakages that occurred, and all of this can impinge on precious time. You need to be friendly but business-like, as you want the property to be ready for the new arrivals.

A well-organised routine will be paramount for changeover day. If you oversee the cleaning yourself but have help, whether they be your partner or a cleaner, you need to ensure that each of you have clearly defined areas to work in and clearly defined duties to perform. This will avoid missing areas or duplicating effort. For example, you may look after the kitchen, dining and living rooms, prepare the welcome basket and tea tray, update instruction leaflets and check information folders. Your cleaner or partner may be responsible for the bedrooms, bathrooms, emptying bins, tidying the garden and fixing any minor maintenance problems.

On changeover day time will be of the essence and you will not want to waste any time by not having the right equipment, cleaning fluids or polishes to hand. You may be able to keep a locked cupboard in the unit, stocked with everything you need for this day, including fresh linen and towels for the beds and bathroom. If you need to bring everything with you, be organised. Time spent in advance getting organised will be time saved on the day itself.

If you live further away and need to employ a caretaker, it will be beneficial to arrange to help occasionally. This way you will be able to reassure yourself that the cleaning is being done efficiently and to your standard.

CLEANING CHECKLIST

It may seem that making beds, dusting, vacuuming and washing are so part of everyday home care that this will not be a problem. But, for the paying guests coming to stay in your self-catering property, every facet of what they use must be perfectly presented in terms of cleanliness. When they enter the property, they really want to feel that no other guest has stayed there previously. Although they will have already gained initial impressions of your property from the enquiry and booking procedures, their first genuine impressions will be when they arrive. Not only will they take into account the visual appearance, but also other senses will come into play such as smell. When guests enter the property you may think they will immediately be wowed by the inglenook fireplace or the view from the window, but if they have sat down on the sofa and found a previous occupant's sock down the side of the cushion or turned on the television and noticed thick white dust, the effect of any adornments that you have added may quickly be lost.

As well as carrying out a thorough clean for any new arrival, you will also need to carry out regular deep-cleaning and periodic spring-cleaning. To help you with all of this, consider using a cleaning checklist. This would detail not only what needs to be cleaned but in which order you need to do it, room by room. Work from top to bottom, from the inside out. You obviously don't want to be emptying bins first when you

Establishing a changeover routine

- DECIDING ON YOUR CHANGEOVER DAY
- WHAT TO DO ON THE DAY
- CLEANING CHECKLIST
- 'DUST MAGNETS' AND 'HIDDEN ZONES'

might be finding litter during the clean, or tidying the garden when you'll be walking mud into the home. The list will also remind you of those areas not to miss. Most will be obvious, such as making the beds, but some may be easily forgotten, such as checking the drawers. How you design the list is up to you. It can vary depending on the property and your management style. But consider using a simple table headed by each room, with areas to be cleaned listed and a check box alongside each area to tick once completed. It may initially seem an additional burden but can prove invaluable when it reminds you to check the drawers and replenish the bath foam.

As time goes by you will get quicker and more efficient on changeover days, but it is still useful to use the checklist as a final walk-through check before closing the front door and welcoming your new arrivals.

Changeover checklist

Sitting room	Done	Bedrooms	Done	Kitchen	Done
All curtains running smoothly	✓	All curtains running smoothly	✓	All blinds/curtains running smoothly	✓
All lamps and bulbs working	✓	All lamps and bulbs working	✓	Check strip lights	✓
Information folders complete	✓	Check radio alarm clocks	✓	Check cutlery drawer for crumbs	✓
Sofa cushions 'out and back'		Drawer liners checked	✓	Check plate stacks	✓
Replace all extras – plants and newspapers	✓	Hangers tidied	✓	Check mug interiors	✓
Check television tuning and the remote control	✓	Tissues replaced	✓	Fingertip-check saucepans	✓

Check clocks	✓	**Bathroom**		Check fridge seals, ice box and ice cube tray	✓
Check smoke alarms (batteries)	✓	Check blinds, curtains, strip lights	✓	Replace foil on cooker tray and grill pan	✓
Shake out rugs	✓	Lock airing cupboard	✓	Check oven clock	✓
Dining room		Replace soaps	✓	Check hob light	✓
All curtains running smoothly	✓	Top up bath foam	✓	Check interior washing machine	✓
All lamps and bulbs working	✓	Sealed cotton wool balls and any extras	✓	Check interior tumble drier	✓
Replace all extras – e.g. plants, flowers	✓	Loo brush (check regularly)	✓	Replace all cleaning cloths	✓
Wipe all table mats/coasters	✓	Toilet roll (remove old rolls)	✓	Replace all extras	✓
Check chair cushions	✓	Check behind the door	✓	Check arrival tray/ welcome basket	✓

'DUST MAGNETS' AND 'HIDDEN ZONES'

Some areas of a property act like magnets for dust. Lampshades will attract dust because of the air movement created by the hot light bulb. A television screen generates static that will draw dust towards it. Curtains are often prone to getting dusty because they are by windows and in air movement.

'Hidden' areas of any accommodation are those areas you don't normally see, such as below a bed, on top of a wardrobe and behind the living room door. It is useful to check these areas on a frequent basis.

The first check

On changeover departure or arrival day, as long as the weather permits, firstly open all of the windows to remove

Establishing a changeover routine

- DECIDING ON YOUR CHANGEOVER DAY
- WHAT TO DO ON THE DAY
- CLEANING CHECKLIST
- 'DUST MAGNETS' AND 'HIDDEN ZONES'

The first check

- KITCHEN
- SITTING AND DINING ROOMS, HALLWAYS AND LANDINGS
- BEDROOMS
- BATHROOM
- OUTSIDE

any stale or lingering smells. This will be more important if you allow pets or smoking in the property. Then work logically through the unit.

KITCHEN

The kitchen can be the most difficult place to clean because it can harbour so many dust and grease 'traps' and invites such close scrutiny from your guests. Some guests have very high expectations of standards of cleanliness and hygiene, and the kitchen will affect their overall impression of your property and your management of it.

The kitchen can require additional attention to detail, so in addition to the points listed below, when you have finished cleaning the kitchen, have one final check of the extractor fan, interior ceiling of the microwave, toaster crumb tray, oven racks and light covers. All can harbour grease, dirt and litter and can be easily forgotten especially when the counter has been wiped, the sink is polished, the windows are sparkling and everything at 'eye level' appears spotless.

Oven – depending on whether or how it has been used there could be grease encrusted on every surface or it may appear untouched. Start by spraying on a cleaner and then leave this for sufficient time for the solution to work whilst you do other things. When you return, the solution should have made clearing any grease or cleaning up burnt spills easy. Don't forget to clean the wire racks and the grill pan. If time allows, or if you have a gap in lettings, you could put shelves and trays through a dishwasher. You could also line the grill pan and baking trays with tin foil to help to cut down on some cleaning.

Hobs and hoods – clean with suitable solutions to bring up a shine and check for burnt-on spills around the burners from pans. Quickly turn on to make sure all rings work. Check the extractor fan and wipe off any grease. A top tip for stainless steel extractor hoods is to give a quick wipe over with baby oil. It prevents any grease from sticking and keeps the hood clean.

Microwaves – because of the way microwaves are used it is very easy for spillages to occur and for splashes to dirty the walls and upper interior surface. Always check these areas as well as cleaning the trays and any microwaveable dishes you have provided.

Washing machine, tumble dryer and dishwasher – open the doors of the washing machine, tumble dryer and dishwasher to air them and check that nothing has been left behind. If you have a dishwasher, you may want to fill it up with crockery and cutlery to give it all a thorough clean. If so, do this first, otherwise you will run out of time. Make sure there are sufficient tablets for the new guests. If you have a washing machine check the washing powder and fabric softener trays as they can get clogged up, and check that there are sufficient supplies of powder and conditioner. With tumble driers, don't forget to check the lint screen.

Fridges and freezers – these need to be checked carefully. Pay special attention to seals and iceboxes as they can collect crumbs and be sure to throw away any remnants of previous occupants' food. Periodically defrost the freezer, but do this during a quiet time.

Work units – wipe down all work surfaces and check all cupboards and drawers. Give extra attention to cutlery trays, which can harbour crumbs, and always remove any leftover food from previous guests.

Crockery, cutlery, utensils and glassware – pay particular attention to crockery, cutlery, utensils and glassware. Black coffee stains in mugs may require soaking and cutlery and utensils may need checking. Carefully check plate stacks; there may be stains on the bottom plate. Glasses may be smeared so it's a good idea to check them carefully and wash any that need cleaning. Remember that you may need to put things back where they belong, especially if you have multi-units where you have let more than one unit to one group.

Pots, pans and ovenware – although these may all appear to be clean, quickly run your hands over them. This will highlight if there are any burnt-on remnants that need extra attention.

The first check

- KITCHEN
- SITTING AND DINING ROOMS, HALLWAYS AND LANDINGS
- BEDROOMS
- BATHROOM
- OUTSIDE

Equipment – check the breadbin and toaster, including the crumb tray, and check for limescale in the kettle – it may need de-scaling periodically, depending on the water hardness in your area.

Extras – you will need to provide a variety of extras, such as light bulbs, washing-up liquid, dishcloths, a dustpan and brush, bin liners and tea towels. Make sure there is a clean supply of everything including cleaning sponges and check any operational instructions for equipment are still where they should be. And don't forget to prepare the welcome tray.

Now methodically work from top to bottom checking and cleaning. Check strip lights (these will often collect insects throughout the course of the year), ledges of high cupboards, blinds (it's a good idea to open them to make sure they work and are not dirty), curtains and windowsills. Work your way down through cupboards and drawers, checking and cleaning. Where necessary, clean windows and finally, empty the kitchen bin and wash the floor, not forgetting the area behind the door.

SITTING AND DINING ROOMS, HALLWAYS AND LANDINGS

As well as needing to empty rubbish bins and remove old newspapers and, if you have one, cleaning out and relaying the fire, you will also need to move some furniture to check for rubbish. Move rugs and seating and pull off loose cushions to check for debris, such as crumbs, toys and coins, and spot clean any stains.

Work around the rooms, again from high to low, checking for cobwebs, dusting ledges and windowsills, and checking curtains. It's a good idea to draw and open these to ensure they have not been pulled off their runners or harbour any marks. Wet wipe coasters, switches or similar surfaces such as lampshades, then dust other surfaces moving all ornaments.

Check that tiebacks on dining seat pads are still intact and then check the television for tuning, and remotes and the smoke alarms for batteries. Set the radiator thermostats and check all light bulbs by quickly turning on all lights. In other areas, such as stairs and landings, you may need to do some high level dusting for cobwebs.

Tidy up any books, games, CDs and videos and throw away any old magazines or replace, as necessary. Then replace any extras, such as a television listings magazine or a box of tissues, and sort through your information folders and replace any missing pages. Then clean the windows and thoroughly vacuum the floors, not forgetting the area behind doors. Finally, leave a vase of flowers.

The first check
- KITCHEN
- SITTING AND DINING ROOMS, HALLWAYS AND LANDINGS
- BEDROOMS
- BATHROOM
- OUTSIDE

BEDROOMS

When cleaning bedrooms (and bathrooms) consider the way in which the guest may use the room. They may be sitting on the bed reading and they will be using the wardrobe to hang their clothes. Their perspective on the room may be slightly different to your own when you are doing the cleaning. Remember that their eye line may reveal the area around the edge of the skirting boards and the often-missed wedge of dust behind the bedroom door when it is closed.

Check all storage areas in case any objects have been left by previous guests, including drawers and wardrobes and the hook on the back of the bedroom door. Ensure that there are still enough hangers in the wardrobes and that drawers are not missing their linings.

Check under the bed and strip and remove dirty linen, checking for staining on mattresses, valances, pillow protectors, duvets and blankets. Remake the beds ensuring that duvet cover fasteners are all in place (fasteners can get damaged during ironing and buttons can come unattached). If you use a laundry for your linen, make sure that there are no tears in it.

Dust, polish and damp clean the rooms working systematically around them working from high to low, and pay special attention to tops of mirrors, picture frames, door tops, headboards, bedside tables, pelmets, curtain tracks and lampshades.

Check any extras, such as bedside lights, radio alarm clocks (make sure the alarm is not set), radiator thermostat valves, curtain hooks and blind pulls. If necessary, clean windows and other glass surfaces and finally thoroughly vacuum the floor.

BATHROOM

As with all other areas of the property, domestic cleaning supplies may suffice for you but commercial brands may be more economical and more effective. This may be especially so in the bathroom, although you may want to consider your environmental policies when purchasing cleaning supplies and select those that are less harmful to the environment.

As with the bedroom, when cleaning the bathroom, consider how the guest uses the room and where their eye line goes. It will often be at low levels, when sitting down or when lying in the bath. At these levels they will notice the underside of the washbasin, the u-bend of the waste pipe, and the edges of the floor. And as with the bedroom, remember to check behind the bathroom door, not just for that wedge of dust that can accumulate, but for also for splashes on the door itself.

The main 'dust magnet' in the bathroom will be the extractor fan. This pulls in dust and can look very unsightly if not cleaned regularly. If you are in a hard water area, keep a careful eye on accumulations of limescale around taps, wastes and shower controls. If any part of the shower tray or bath contains sitting water this may also lead to a build-up of limescale.

Your cleaning schedule should include removing and replenishing all towelling and soaps and topping up any bottled toiletries, such as bath foam. Then clean from high to low, cleaning the extractor fan, shower and bath, washbasin, toilet and walls. Remove dust from the extractor fan with the long nozzle or brush of the vacuum and check carefully for mould or mildew on tiles and shower curtains. You may need to replace the curtain on a regular basis. Check for hair in plugs and corners and edges of the shower. Do the same for the washbasin, checking for toothpaste, soap and make-up residue. Polish the taps, and clean, dry and polish glass screens and mirrors.

Clean and brush the toilet bowl with an appropriate cleaner, especially under the rim, and flush and disinfect to leave it looking and smelling clean. Clean the seat and lid and dry and ensure the toilet brush is clean and placed in its container.

Replenish toilet rolls and leave a clean cloth for wiping over the bath, empty the rubbish bin and finally clean the floor, not forgetting the area behind the bathroom door, and wipe the door handle.

Doing such a thorough clean each changeover day will become routine and relatively quick, but it's really worth giving cleanliness in the bathroom extra attention to detail.

OUTSIDE

Depending on your property, you may have very little to attend to outside or you may need a lot of time to tend to the exterior, grounds and garden of your property. Indeed, you may need to cut the grass and do gardening on another day.

Whatever type of property you have you will need to check that the dustbin has not been left overflowing (you may have to take some refuse away) and possibly sweep paths, check external light bulbs, and clean the outside of windows.

Additional cleaning and maintenance

In addition to the weekly changeover, some guests may stay for more than one week or you may have decided to take long lets during the quiet season, which will require a different cleaning schedule. You will also need to carry out regular deep cleans and maintenance checks throughout the year.

LONGER STAYS

For guests staying longer than a week, you will need to decide on a cleaning policy and whether you will offer to have the unit cleaned and linen changed midway through their stay. Guests may not want to be disturbed and might be happy to change the linen themselves, so you will need to make certain that you have sufficient sets available.

The first check

- KITCHEN
- SITTING AND DINING ROOMS, HALLWAYS AND LANDINGS
- BEDROOMS
- BATHROOM
- OUTSIDE

Additional cleaning and maintenance

- LONGER STAYS
- DEEP CLEANS
- REPLACEMENTS

Arrangements to carry out cleaning may be more complicated. You may be able to do this yourself at a pre-arranged time, or if you have to wait until the end of their stay, you may need an extra pair of hands on changeover day as the property may need extra cleaning.

DEEP CLEANS

In addition to the weekly changeover routine, you will need to carry out a deeper clean on a regular basis. Some areas and items may only require annual attention, such as sweeping the chimney, but for others areas you will need to judge the frequency according to occupancy levels and wear and tear.

Furniture may need moving for all-round vacuuming, paintwork may need touching up, mattresses will require vacuuming, flipping and turning (try to do this every three months, if possible) and duvets and blankets will need to be dry cleaned. If you provide seasonal tog rating duvets, you may be better doing this during a quieter period.

Curtains, nets and voiles may require regular washing, carpets can be shampooed and loose covers on furniture dry cleaned. If you allow pets, be prepared for extra cleaning, especially for carpets and soft furnishings. Washing all windows inside and outside may be a regular job, and general ongoing maintenance will be required, such as redecoration (also for inside and out), bleeding radiators and servicing electrical appliances, boilers and gas fires.

In gardens you will need to assess if you will have sufficient time during weekly changeovers to maintain lawns and planting. You may decide that additional hard landscaping, such as a deck or patio, will be more effective and suit guests' needs better.

If you employ a cleaner, it can be useful to identify a daily cleaning schedule, a weekly schedule, a monthly schedule and a quarterly schedule to cover all the areas detailed above.

REPLACEMENTS

Although you will keep a small supply of replacements for breakages or stained items, you will also need to regularly renew items such as kitchen utensils, cutlery, tablemats, crockery and serving dishes, pillows, mattresses and pillow protectors, bed linen, cushions, seat pads, lampshades and toilet brushes. The list is longer than that given here, and some items will need replacing more frequently than others. For example, non-stick frying pans can get damaged very quickly and may need replacing more frequently than non-stick saucepans. The important point is to try to keep everything you provide in good condition. As a consequence, it can sometimes be prudent to purchase more expensive items that will be more durable than less expensive items that will need to be replaced more frequently.

Additional cleaning and maintenance

- LONGER STAYS

- DEEP CLEANS

- REPLACEMENTS

Test your property

Test your property

As highlighted in Chapter 3, 'Equipping the unit', you should spend at least one night in your property and use the bedrooms, bathroom and all facilities yourself on an annual basis. By doing this you will be able to assess how well your property or units function and decide whether you need to make any fine-tune changes to the design, location of furniture or add some more 'extras'. You may get friends or family to use your accommodation when staying. If so, get them to give feedback on noise levels, 'ease of use', and any aspect that could enhance the property. It may be something as simple as a larger clock in the living room, a wider door hinge on a kitchen unit or the addition of some DVDs for the new DVD player you installed.

Sleeping in your own accommodation can be considered as an annual self-assessment, not just to see how easy it is for guests to use your property but, more importantly, to assess if wear and tear is creeping into areas you would not normally notice – does the oven timer still function, does the bathroom extractor fan still work effectively, and is the bed mattress still firm? Carrying out this self-assessment can be an eye-opener and, as highlighted in Chapter 3, a room-by-room checklist will help you quickly identify priorities for future quality development, highlighting aspects you may need to address in the coming year.

Next chapter

In the next chapter we look at ways in which you can start to grow your business. We will look at what you should be doing to track your business through your first full season of trading and how you could use this information to help formulate ideas for continued growth. Even if you have found the year very busy, it is still important to know how business came to you, what advertising worked and if there may be other ways to stimulate business. Being busy today is not always a guarantee of being busy tomorrow.

Chapter 9
Growing your business

Having set up your self-catering property and worked hard to prepare and equip it, implemented an advertising campaign, met your guests and organised an efficient cleaning routine, you now need to review the first year. The biggest question to ask yourself will be whether you have enjoyed the experience. There may have been some difficult points or challenging situations, but hopefully you will have met many pleasant and interesting people and can reflect on how much your hard work has contributed towards the enjoyment of their holiday.

Step 1 – Review the year

As with all projects you cannot sit back and rest on your laurels. You need to look back and assess if and where you should make changes. Did you make the right decision in agreeing to take pets, or has it resulted in a lot of additional cleaning? Should you try to aim for a different type of market in the future? Were many enquiries looking for a facility that you did not have, and as a consequence did you lose bookings? Did you get many bookings from your advertising or were some adverts non-productive? Feedback from your guests can be invaluable in helping you to assess what you are doing right as well as if there is anything you are doing wrong.

EVALUATING FEEDBACK
Many self-catering properties have a guests' comment book. This is a good way of getting feedback, as many guests are happy to record a few thoughts at the end of their stay. It is also a pleasant way for you to read how much they enjoyed

Step 1 – Review the year

- EVALUATING FEEDBACK
- HOW DID YOUR GUESTS FIND YOUR PROPERTY?
- KEEPING IN TOUCH

staying with you and you will almost certainly receive many pleasant comments. However, it can also be useful to know more specifically how their stay was. Was the bed comfortable, did the lighting work or was the cottage too noisy? A guest feedback book or card can be used to find out if everything worked well, if the room was easy to use and whether there could have been anything else to enhance their stay. Not every guest will complete it but, from the ones that do, you'll quickly build up a clear picture of how they really see your property.

Another good question to ask is what they liked the most about the property. This will highlight what the most special feature or most memorable part of the property was. It can be surprising what guests say. It may not be the fact you have a swimming pool or have put in a widescreen television, but instead may be the view from the bedroom window of the birds on the bird feeder. We'll see why this information is so important shortly, but it will often highlight that what you may feel is special about your property may not match your guests' idea of what's special.

HOW DID YOUR GUESTS FIND YOUR PROPERTY?

This is an important question that you should try to ask each guest at the outset. You should ask the question at the time of booking or on the booking form, and keep a record after asking so you can accurately track how business came to you.

KEEPING IN TOUCH

The best form of business is repeat business, but how do you keep these guests returning? For guests who you have a good rapport with and for the ones you'd enjoy returning, you could consider sending a Christmas card or even a New Year card. The latter can be useful as it is more likely to be kept after the Christmas cards have been discarded. But do remember, sending cards is not suitable or necessary for all guests.

Step 2 – Developing yourself and your property

Guest expectations are continually increasing and in order for your business to stand out you need to think of how you can adapt, so that you do not miss out. Now that your business is up and running it's a good time to think about what you can do to improve both your own management skills and the appeal of your property.

DEVELOPING YOURSELF

Learning new skills can, even within a small business such as self-catering, contribute significantly to developing your business. Contact your local Tourist Information Centre or tourist organisation for advice on suitable courses in your area. They may be able to put you in touch with your local Tourism Officer, or regional tourist board, or the tourism section of your regional development agency. Many of these organisations coordinate, or have knowledge of a variety of courses throughout the year designed specifically for smaller tourism businesses. Courses can cover disability awareness, brochure design, bookkeeping skills and the Welcome to Excellence family of courses. The Welcome courses are an excellent way to develop your understanding of customer care.

DEVELOPING YOUR PROPERTY

After your first year of operation and after the first quality assessment you should consider whether the overall quality of your property and the grade achieved could be developed. Use the assessor's visit and their guidance to consider if you could develop higher quality standards, but don't go chasing ratings for the sake of it. Quality development should be done to match guests' needs and raise your profile accordingly. Planned quality development can sometimes lead to business development.

ENHANCE YOUR RATING

If, at the time of your assessment, you were advised you were close to a higher quality grade, then consider whether reaching that grade will be beneficial for your business. Sometimes it may not. Consider a 4-star self-catering property close to achieving 5 stars. Five stars is the highest rating you can have, but at that level guests may have very high expectations. If you match or exceed those expectations then the guest should be happy. But if you miss them, they

---

Step 1 – Review the year

- EVALUATING FEEDBACK
- HOW DID YOUR GUESTS FIND YOUR PROPERTY?
- KEEPING IN TOUCH

Step 2 – Developing yourself and your property

- DEVELOPING YOURSELF
- DEVELOPING YOUR PROPERTY
- ENHANCE YOUR RATING
- MEETING NEEDS AND BEING DISTINCTIVE
- DEVELOPING A MORE ACCESSIBLE SELF-CATERING PROPERTY
- NATIONAL ACCESSIBLE SCHEME

may be disappointed. Sometimes, promising less but delivering more can work better and being at the top end of one star band, rather than at the lower end of another, can be beneficial.

MEETING NEEDS AND BEING DISTINCTIVE

The use of the feedback form can be used to very good effect. You may have started your self-catering business expecting lots of guests on holiday and have furnished and styled your accommodation accordingly. Now, after a full season or year in business, you may realise that many of your guests are actually working in the area with quite different requirements to holidaymakers. Did you attract those families you expected or did you find that there were more activity guests and your children's room with bunk beds was rarely required?

The feedback forms may help you decide if you need to restyle your accommodation, add anything or even remove items. If you have many guests walking or birdwatching, you may now realise that a more extensive range of OS maps, a spare pair of binoculars and offering to tumble dry wet clothes are useful extras.

Maybe you could offer a dinner delivery service, especially for the first night. Not many properties will have their own leisure activities but perhaps you could arrange sporting activities such as clay shooting or gym membership with local clubs. If you have created a number of units or converted redundant buildings, you may have sufficient space to have a dedicated play barn equipped with table tennis, darts or a pool table.

DEVELOPING A MORE ACCESSIBLE SELF-CATERING PROPERTY

In Chapter 2 we highlighted various laws that could affect how you operate your self-catering business. One such law is the Disability Discrimination Act (DDA). Accessibility is nothing new. Numerous operators have complied within the spirit of the DDA for many years, by adapting their properties to cater for guests with disabilities. They have done this to meet the needs of the market. Meeting the needs of the DDA is a legal requirement, but it can also be good for your business.

Consider the following facts:

There are 9 million disabled people in this country – 1 in 6 of us.

- 2.7 million disabled people regularly travel in this country and they travel with friends, with family and with carers. The entire market contains over 15 million people, a quarter of the population.
- It is estimated that the market has a spending power of over £50 billion.
- 5% of disabled people are in wheelchairs.
- Only 12% of us have 20:20 vision.
- Half of all disabled people in the UK are over 65.
- By 2011 30% of the population will be over 55.
- The over 50s possess 80% of the UK wealth.

Much of the symbolism used to denote the disabled market uses the wheelchair symbol, but disabilities are varied and include learning disabilities, blindness, loss of hearing, arthritis, asthma and diabetes. Millions of people have a temporary disability, such as pregnant mothers and people with injuries. The disabled market is a strong market and research shows that disabled travellers are loyal customers.

NATIONAL ACCESSIBLE SCHEME

VisitBritain's National Accessible Scheme (NAS) recognises and identifies self-catering properties which meet the needs of guests with disabilities.

The NAS assesses the suitability of accommodation against three types of disability: mobility, sight and hearing. The scheme contains a standard for each type of disability and you can achieve a rating to help promote your business more readily to the disabled market. For mobility there are four ratings that can be achieved, for sight two ratings and for hearing also two ratings. It may be that you cannot achieve a rating against all of the standards nor attain the highest rating within each standard, but you might be able to meet some of the standards for some of the schemes. There will always be

Step 2 – Developing yourself and your property

- DEVELOPING YOURSELF
- DEVELOPING YOUR PROPERTY
- ENHANCE YOUR RATING
- MEETING NEEDS AND BEING DISTINCTIVE
- DEVELOPING A MORE ACCESSIBLE SELF-CATERING PROPERTY
- NATIONAL ACCESSIBLE SCHEME

some adaptations you can make. To aid you further there is a self-assessment pack which accompanies the standards. This allows you to assess your own property against the three standards and helps you to formulate an action plan for future developments.

For further information on the National Accessible Scheme please contact Quality in Tourism on 0845 3006996 or e-mail qualityintourism@gslglobal.com.

Step 3 – Repeats and referrals

Repeat business can be the best type of business, but after that, the next best can be recommended and referral business. If your guest has had a good stay they will hopefully recommend you to friends, family and colleagues.

REPEAT BOOKINGS

Hopefully you will start to receive repeat bookings from your first year, although this may not always happen. Repeat visitors often have a pattern of revisiting every three or more years, so do not be disheartened in your second year if they do not book again. New business always means that these guests could also be repeats in future years.

To tempt repeat visitors, you could consider offering a discount, especially if they book early. Although more and more people make last-minute decisions on holidays and short breaks, there are still those who make plans as soon as Christmas is over. From your records you will have the names and addresses of those who have stayed. As highlighted above, consider sending out a New Year card but include an early booking offer or an availability listing. If you have your own website or belong to an association, do not forget to amend your details with any discounts.

REFERRAL BUSINESS

Referral business can come from other self-catering properties. We mentioned in Chapter 2 the idea of contacting other self-catering properties in your area, as you get ready to launch your business. If a more formal association exists, consider joining them. The opportunities of meeting other like-minded people who are having similar experiences to you will prove invaluable. You will be able to swap notes, compare bookings and pick up new ideas. Local associations can help you realise if you are not as busy as everyone else and possibly missing an opportunity. You may be able to visit other properties in the association and realise where you fit in to the local picture.

Being able to visit other local self-catering properties can also be very useful should you receive an enquiry for a period when you are already full. If you know your colleagues, you can refer calls with confidence, knowing your guests will get a similar experience to if they had stayed with you. And this works for your colleagues. If they know your property and the style and size of your accommodation, they can also refer business to you, with added confidence and reassurance.

Local associations can also be a very useful way of bulk-purchasing various items such as toiletries and other accessories, thereby reducing your outgoings.

Step 4 – Raising your profile locally

Raising your profile locally may seem a strange idea. After all, you are trying to get guests to stay from a long distance away, not from your own doorstep, but the local market can prove very fruitful.

LOCAL OPPORTUNITIES

Guests visiting friends and relations for longer than a weekend may consider self-catering as an alternative to a B&B or hotel. It is good practice to be known locally to capture this business. Consider advertising in a local parish or village magazine, or local newspaper.

Similarly, people moving home may want to stay in an area to see if it suits them. Visit your local estate agents and see if they would welcome passing on your details. Consider also any events that may bring people to your area. For example, there may be a company that plans weddings, a wedding cake maker or caterers. All may receive requests from the wedding party for advice on places to stay and some may welcome your details.

Step 2 – Developing yourself and your property
- DEVELOPING YOURSELF
- DEVELOPING YOUR PROPERTY
- ENHANCE YOUR RATING
- MEETING NEEDS AND BEING DISTINCTIVE
- DEVELOPING A MORE ACCESSIBLE SELF-CATERING PROPERTY
- NATIONAL ACCESSIBLE SCHEME

Step 3 – Repeats and referrals
- REPEAT BOOKINGS
- REFERRAL BUSINESS

Step 4 – Raising your profile locally
- LOCAL OPPORTUNITIES
- MAKE FRIENDS WITH YOUR TIC
- THE BUSINESS MARKET

MAKE FRIENDS WITH YOUR TIC

The local Tourist Information Centre is going to be a very useful point of contact for you. You may not realise how effective they can be in promoting your property. They may, or may not, generate bookings but the exposure they provide can be invaluable. During the course of the year they may have sent you a number of guests, but even if they have not, you should build a close relationship with them. To help them match suitable properties to the enquiries they receive, consider inviting the staff round, or take in some photographs of your property so they can see what it looks like. Keep them advised on availability and go to any open days or leaflet swaps they organise.

THE BUSINESS MARKET

Depending on your location, the travelling business market is another area that can provide you with accommodation bookings. It can be useful to identify any local companies that need accommodation for staff attending their offices for meetings or training courses. The opportunities for attracting the business market can be quite significant in some areas. Consider contacting various companies to enquire if they ever require longer stay accommodation for staff. It is no good sending your details to the Managing Director if it is the head of personnel who makes the bookings, so try to find out who is responsible for making bookings and then send them your details.

Also, think about contacting training schools, colleges and universities that bring in specialist tutors and trainers for short periods during term times. They will often need accommodation for blocks of one to two weeks and could provide you with useful business out of the main holiday season.

Step 5 – Developing your marketing

You may have started marketing and promoting your property by creating a simple brochure and then during the year you may have placed an advertisement in a local magazine. Now that your business is beginning to move forward, it could be worth thinking about new marketing ideas.

DEVELOPING YOUR BROCHURE

Design ideas for a brochure were covered in Chapter 5 but it is now worth considering how well your brochure works and whether it needs changing. Brochures can be professionally printed and the photographs taken by a commercial photographer, or you could develop one yourself by using a digital camera and an office stationery company. However, creating a brochure that really sells your property will need impact. Think about the feedback you had from guests about what they thought was the most special or memorable aspect of your property. It may have been the kitchen, the living room or the garden. It is said that a picture is worth a thousand words, so include photographs of those aspects. It may be important to show a number of features including the frontage of the house, the rooms and the garden. But based on the feedback you receive, you may want to include a photograph of the view out of the bedroom window, or even yourself! Consider using one main image within the brochure and select the image that possibly best sums up your self-catering property.

If you have developed a website, add the web address to the new brochure, and don't forget to promote your quality rating.

DEVELOPING A WEBSITE

If you do not have a website, now may be the time to consider developing one. It need not be expensive and you may even consider building it yourself. With your own website you can update information immediately, refresh photographs as the seasons or property changes and show your property in much more detail than in a brochure.

If you have been assessed by VisitBritain you will receive free entry onto www.visitbritain.org, the official tourism website for England. This in turn can provide a direct link to your own website. Alternatively, if developing a website is going to prove too expensive, find out the costs of being included on a local accommodation association site.

Step 4 – Raising your profile locally

- LOCAL OPPORTUNITIES
- MAKE FRIENDS WITH YOUR TIC
- THE BUSINESS MARKET

Step 5 – Developing your marketing

- DEVELOPING YOUR BROCHURE
- DEVELOPING A WEBSITE
- ADVERTISING
- SPECIAL OFFERS
- PLAN THE YEAR

ADVERTISING

One of the benefits of being assessed by VisitBritain is a free listing in the *Where to Stay* guides, which have international distribution. This may provide you with all the exposure you need, or you may decide you need to advertise elsewhere as well.

Advertising in local accommodation or regional guides may be useful. You can visit your Tourist Information Centre for more advice on local guides. If you know a significant proportion of your visitors come from a certain geographical area, obtain that local newspaper and consider advertising in that. They may regularly carry features on your region and may even have a special advertising rate.

Advertising elsewhere can be expensive, especially for smaller businesses, but it may be necessary. Advertising must be truthful (bear in mind the Trade Descriptions Act) but with any advertising you need to create awareness of your property by conveying information that produces interest and appeal. Use your rating; it can attract attention quickly and highlights that you have an official endorsement. Above all, have a budget and stick to it, but be aware that a single advertisement is unlikely to have a great impact and the effect of advertising can be cumulative, so it may need repeating.

You need to keep a track of all costings to evaluate what has been effective. Consider creating a spreadsheet and list the calendar months across the top. In the left column list all the publications that you have paid to advertise in and slot in under the months how many bookings you have received from each advert. From this you can compare what your total spend per publication was against the number of bookings you received. For example, if you spent £300.00 to advertise in a guide and received five bookings you know that each booking cost you £60.00. However, you may find that an advert in a parish magazine cost £25.00 for the year, and that also gave you five bookings, costing £5.00 per booking. Then total up all your bookings for the year (including those from other sources, such as friends and recommendations) against your total advertising costs. This will show the actual cost per booking. When you started your business you may have predicted a target cost for each booking. By compiling this spreadsheet you will be able to evaluate how near you were to budget. This exercise will then give you an overview of where you may want to advertise in the future.

Step 5 – Developing your marketing

- DEVELOPING YOUR BROCHURE
- DEVELOPING A WEBSITE
- ADVERTISING
- SPECIAL OFFERS
- PLAN THE YEAR

SPECIAL OFFERS

Depending on your business and the pattern of bookings throughout the year you could consider special offers to encourage bookings. This could include a late deal to fill an empty week or a midweek four-night stay for the same price as three. If you decide to offer special deals and have a website, you will be able to update any offers on a daily basis. Otherwise you may need to consider additional advertising to promote the offer.

PLAN THE YEAR

It is very useful to prepare a marketing/advertising calendar so that you can plan your year and spread your costs. Mark months with relevant activity to be sure you don't miss deadlines. Regional and local accommodation guides tend to go to the printers in the autumn to be ready for distribution before the end of the year. As a consequence, information is usually collected in the summer and, if you want to be included, you'll have to get your entry in by then. This will usually include a fee, so if you have a set budget for the year, and want to spread costs out, highlight this as being a high-cost month.

Find out about annual events, festivals and activities, such as county shows, motor racing and trade fairs, and mark these on your calendar. You may want to contact the organisers or promoters of the event and find out how they advertise it. You could possibly advertise in their programme, which could be another way of publicising your business, or obtain a list of exhibitors or trade stands who will be in need of accommodation. They may not want a full week and you will naturally not take a two-night midweek stay right in the height of the season, but there may be possibilities in the shoulder or low season.

Step 6 – Agencies

Over the first year of business you will have been reviewing your marketing, maintenance and bookings and have an overview of the management of your property or properties. This is a good time to ask yourself whether you have enjoyed running your own business, working from home and meeting your guests. Have you found it difficult to cope with changeover days, do you feel that you have no free time anymore and are you unable to take holidays or make social arrangements? If the answer is yes, then you might want to think about alternative methods of managing your property, such as agencies and property management companies.

WHAT DO AGENCIES DO?

Most agencies will market the property through their brochures and website, oversee all the administration, manage bookings and deal with letting contracts, payments and cancellations. Some also employ cleaners or a caretaker to look after the property whilst occupied and manage changeover day. They will usually visit your property before accepting you onto their books and, according to its location, sleeping accommodation, range of facilities and general quality standard, will agree a designated price band for it to be let at. They will then pay you the rental less a commission fee.

HOW DO I CHOOSE AN AGENCY?

Agencies will vary in what they offer owners, so you will need to do some research before deciding firstly whether you are making the right decision, and secondly, which agency to choose.

Some agencies cover the whole country, whilst others will specialise in specific geographical regions. Some may be very selective and only take on properties at the 'luxury' end of the market. Some may charge an annual registration fee and many will put restrictions on when you can have the property for your own use. Agencies can offer advice on taxation and law, and arrange insurance coverage. In return, you might be committed to a one- or two-year contract, and there could be a significant penalty if you decide to terminate the agreement.

In order for you to choose the right agency for your property, look through the holiday sections of newspapers and magazines and request their brochures. As you did research on other self-catering properties, so do the same research on agencies. It will be useful for you to see the guides they send out on request to see how well they promote properties and how efficiently they deal with enquiries.

Step 6 – Agencies

- WHAT DO AGENCIES DO?

- HOW DO I CHOOSE AN AGENCY?

Consider how their brochure is presented and how easy it is to read and understand from a guest's perspective. Are there detailed descriptions and colour photographs or line drawings? Is the website well designed and easy to navigate? Does it contain additional photographs and enhanced information? Is the website easily found on a search engine? And, can bookings be made online?

Then approach the agencies. Find out whether there is a registration fee, how much it is and whether it is a one-off or an annual payment. How do they promote their brochures, are they published annually and when? Can the agency guarantee a certain number of weeks for you and how many weeks will you be allowed to use your property or are there various restrictions on when you can have it? Can you let the property yourself, or will the agency have an exclusive arrangement? If you take bookings do you have to pay the fee that they would have received if they had taken the booking? Do they offer discounts, and if so, will you be bearing the cost? Will they oversee changeover days and will they meet the visitors? What happens should there be a complaint? Will the agency deal with it? Are they contactable 24 hours a day and what happens in the case of an emergency? Do they make recommendations and give advice on upgrading and improving the property?

As you can see, handing the management of your property over to an agency needs to be carefully considered to ensure it is the right decision for you. It can be a very good idea, especially if you are distant from your property, are unable to make much use of it for most of the year or have just started and are having difficulty getting bookings.

Alternatively, if you are able to handle the administration, marketing and booking arrangements you may only need the services of a property management company. They may be able to offer a personalised service which can include housekeeping, gardening, laundry and linen hire, weekly property checks when its unoccupied, meeting guests on arrival and provide 24-hour emergency cover.

Next chapter

In the next and final chapter we look at problems and solutions. For most self-catering operators their businesses run smoothly, but every now and again you may have to confront a situation for which there is no immediate or obvious solution. The next chapter looks at a variety of situations and offers guidance on how to handle them. We also give a useful list containing sources of further help and the various tourism bodies that can help you on your way.

Chapter 10
Dealing with problems

This short chapter could never cover every eventuality, but it highlights some of the areas that seem to arise occasionally with operators and examines options for prevention as well as cure. Following that, there are some contact details of various organisations that you may want to approach for further advice and guidance on setting up your self-catering business.

Problems and solutions

It is true to say that with most well managed self-catering properties, problems are the exception rather than the rule.

RECEIVING COMPLAINTS

Naturally you hope that everyone who stays in your property will enjoy themselves, that all the equipment works and that the weather remains good for the duration of your guests' stay. Sadly, though, the very nature of the business you are in may mean that there will be the occasional time when things go wrong.

It may not be as a direct result of anything that is lacking with the accommodation, but may often be as a consequence of something totally unconnected. A difficult journey to your property, roadworks, diversions, a car full of fretful children or a delay in leaving can all result in the best of guests arriving in a bad frame of mind. Alternatively, they may find that the dishwasher is faulty and they are unable to use it for the rest of the week. Whatever the problem, you will need to handle the situation with diplomacy and care.

HOW TO DEAL WITH PROBLEMS

It may be difficult not to take complaints personally, but try to be objective. First, always be courteous and listen to what it being said no matter how unjustified you feel the complaint is. Try not to interject with a counter-argument before you have heard their side, and remember there are always two sides to every complaint.

By listening and not interrupting you will at least make them realise that you are taking the issue seriously. Body language will be important. Any gestures could either inflame the situation or help to diffuse it. If necessary, ask the guest to go somewhere that is private, so that any discussions are not audible to other guests or family members. A polite complaint will usually give you the opportunity to rectify a situation.

With any unpredictable problem, such as a faulty boiler or burst water pipes, you, or your cleaner or caretaker, will need to assess the problem and take corrective action. Obviously your insurance company must be advised of such situations, but depending on the severity of the problem you may want to offer a token gesture such as a bunch of flowers, chocolates or wine to cover your guests' inconvenience. Do not offer money as this can become complicated and be seen as an admission of guilt. Most people will be understanding and realise that unforeseen emergencies do, albeit on very rare occasions, happen.

If the complaint is completely out of your control, such as a local swimming pool being closed when all the promotional information indicated it should be open, all you can do is apologise. This will not resolve the complaint, but at least the guest will realise that you are concerned.

You may also receive a complaint letter after guests have left. Any complaint made after guests have left will not be so easy to remedy but should always receive a written response.

If you let your property through an agency make sure that you are aware of the terms and conditions on the agency agreement. Often an agency may initially respond to the complaint, but ultimately the contract is between the hirer and yourself and you may eventually have to deal with it. Just remember not to ever ignore a complaint.

Finally, adopt as many as possible of the suggestions made within this book to your guests' needs and exceed their expectations. Those guests who did have a bad journey to you will be uplifted to find the property warm, lamps left on and a welcome basket in the kitchen. Those who could not visit a swimming pool because it was closed will be pleased by the helpful advice you put together in your information folders.

Problems and solutions

- RECEIVING COMPLAINTS
- HOW TO DEAL WITH PROBLEMS
- DAMAGE TO, OR LOSS OF, YOUR PROPERTY AND POSSESSIONS

DAMAGE TO, OR LOSS OF, YOUR PROPERTY AND POSSESSIONS

As with life, accidents will happen in your property. If a guest breaks an ornament or knocks a bedside light over, this will be part of the expected wear and tear of operating a self-catering business. Often, guests will let you know if they have broken something, but sometimes they will be too embarrassed to say anything and you will not find out until changeover day (just one of the reasons for checking that everything is working when you clean the property).

There may be an occasion when something is broken or damaged that you feel you cannot ignore. Your insurance policy may cover you for some situations, such as a flood caused by a running tap and water damage to flooring. However, there may also be the occasion when you discover damage, such as an iron mark on the carpet, after the guest has paid and departed. In these situations, you should contact the guest immediately and then follow up the call with an invoice and a quotation for the cost of the repair or replacement of the item.

A similar procedure could follow where something is missing. Theft from self-catering properties is very rare and if it does occur, you may want to contact the police. However, it may be that something has been taken inadvertently, such as a map or bath towels. If this happens, contact the guest and first see if the item can be found and returned.

In both of the above situations, if the matter does not resolve itself quickly, then you could decide on taking legal action. This is a very difficult decision to take, as it can become protracted, but that is a decision you will have to make.

Ultimately, depending upon the situation, you may decide the best course of action is to absorb any cost and carry on, putting the matter behind you.

By acknowledging that there can be some common problems, we are not saying that these are everyday ones. The day-to-day running of England's self-catering properties follows a successful formula that is based on genuine hospitality enjoyed by thousands of delighted guests each year. If you are one of the happy band of operators you will know what the rewards can be, especially when you can tap into a good market. If you are about to embark on a new venture, good luck. We hope that this guide has given you a helpful insight.

Sources of further help

There are various organisations responsible for managing tourism in England, from VisitBritain, who cover all of England, to the regional tourist boards, who cover their respective regions. However, your first point of contact should always be your local or nearest tourist information centre. Tourist information centres (sometimes called 'visitor information centres') operate at a local level and should be able to put you in touch with a local, district or county tourism officer. Your tourism officer may be able to give you the best advice on local tourism matters including any tourism initiatives, local associations and groups, and local or regional guides and publications.

Useful contacts

Below are listed the main tourism-related organisations in England.

National Tourist Board

VisitBritain
Thames Tower
Black's Road
London W6 9EL
Tel: 020 8846 9000
Fax: 020 8563 0302
www.visitbritain.com
www.visitengland.com

National Quality Assurance Schemes

For information on how to join the National Quality Assurance Schemes contact:

Quality in Tourism
Farncombe House
Farncombe
Broadway
WR12 7LJ
Tel: 0845 300 6996
Fax: 01386 854319
www.qualityintourism.co.uk

Regional Tourist Boards

Northumbria
One NorthEast Tourism Team
Stella House
Goldcrest Way
Newburn Riverside
Newcastle upon Tyne
NE15 8NY
www.tourismnortheast.co.uk

North West
Cumbria Tourist Board
Ashleigh
Holly Road
Windermere
LA23 2AQ
Tel: 015394 4444
Fax: 015394 44041
www.cumbriatourism.info

Lancashire & Blackpool Tourist Board
St George's House
St George's Street
Chorley
PR7 2AA
www.lancashiretourism.com

Marketing Manchester
Churchgate House
56 Oxford Street
Manchester
M1 6EU
www.destinationmanchester.com

The Mersey Partnership
12 Princes Dock
Princes Parade
Liverpool
L3 1BG
www.visitliverpool.com

Cheshire & Warrington Tourism Board
Grosvenor Park Lodge
Grosvenor Park Road
Chester
CH1 1QQ
www.visit-cheshire.com

Yorkshire

Yorkshire Tourist Board
312 Tadcaster Rd
York
YO24 1GS
Tel: 01904 702 000
Fax: 01904 701 414
www.yorkshiretouristboard.net

East Midlands

East Midlands Tourism
Apex Court
City Link
Nottingham
NG2 4LA
www.emda.org.uk/tourism/tourism

West Midlands

Heart of England Tourism
Woodside
Larkhill Road
Worcester
WR5 2EZ
www.hetb.co.uk

East of England

East of England Tourist Board
Toppesfield Hall
Hadleigh
Suffolk
IP7 5DN
Tel: 01473 822922
Fax: 01473 823063
www.eetb.org.uk

London

London Tourist Board & Convention Board
1 Warwick Row
London
SW1E 5ER
Tel: 020 7932 2000
Fax: 020 7932 0222
www.visitlondon.com

South East

Tourism South East
40 Chamberlayne Road
Eastleigh
Hampshire
SO50 5JH
www.tourismse.com

South West

South West Tourism
Woodwater Park
Pynes Hill
Exeter
EX2 5WT
Tel: 0870 442 0830
Fax: 0870 442 0840
www.swtourism.co.uk

The Pink Booklet

For advice on all legal aspects affecting setting up and
operating a self-catering property you may want to consult
the Pink Booklet. The Pink Booklet is available from
VisitBritain on 0870 606 7204.

Disability Discrimination Act (DDA)

For more information on the Disability Discrimination Act and
help with good business practice contact the Disability Rights
Commission's (DRC) helpline on 08457 622 633 (text phone
08457 622 644). The DRC's websites are www.drc-gb.org
and www.open4all.org

DRC Helpline
FREEPOST
MID 02164
Stratford upon Avon
CV37 9BR

Holiday Care is the national charity offering a central source
of travel and holiday information for disabled, older people
and carers.

Holiday Care
7th Floor
Sunley House
4 Bedford Park
Croydon
Surrey CR0 2AP

Tel: 0845 124 9974
Fax: 0845 124 9972
www.holidaycare.org.uk

Associations

There are many accommodation associations and groups
around the country who can offer support when setting
up a new self-catering operation. One of the largest groups
in England is Farm Stay UK and if you are a working farm
they may be a useful organisation to contact.

Farm Stay UK Ltd
National Agricultural Centre
Stoneleigh Park
Warwickshire
CV8 2LG
Tel: 024 7669 6909
Fax: 024 7669 6630
www.farmstayuk.co.uk

English Association of Self-Catering Operators
Toad Hall Cottages
Elliott House
73 Church Street
Kingsbridge
TQ7 1BY
Tel: 01548 852407
Fax: 01548 853086
www.englishselfcatering.co.uk

Index